# CLASSIC BUS

## YEARBOOK – 4

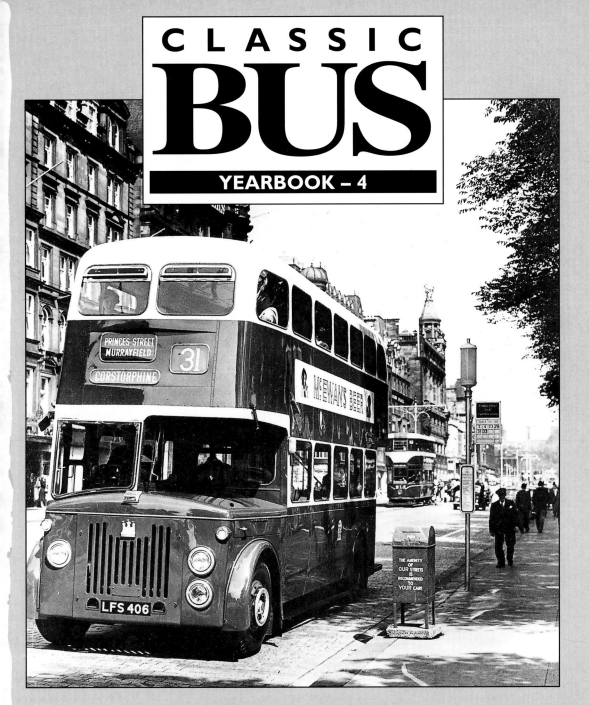

EDITED BY GAVIN BOOTH

**IAN ALLAN** *Publishing*

# CONTENTS

First published 1998

ISBN 0 7110 2584 3

Design by Hieroglyph

Published by Ian Allan Publishing an imprint of Ian Allan Ltd, Terminal House, Station Approach, Shepperton, Surrey TW17 8AS Printed by Ian Allan Printing Ltd, River Dene Estate, Hersham, Surrey KT12 4RG

Code: 9804/B2

# INTRODUCTION

THE NOSTALGIA for the buses of our younger days seems to grow stronger as the years and the waistlines advance. Nostalgia is an essential ingredient in *Classic Bus Yearbook*, now in its fourth annual edition. Every reader should relate to some of the contributions in the book – whether it's Michael Baker recalling the wonderful variety of coaches that thronged London's Victoria Coach Station in the 1950s, or Brian Parkin on Leeds' flirtation with two-door buses, or Nigel Furness on the pleasures of Bristol's buses 30 years ago, or David Thrower waxing philosophical about the dwindling band of classics in the Greater Manchester fleet.

Michael Yelton took a Southdown timetable as his holiday reading, and marvels at the travel opportunities offered, directly and through carefully-planned connections. Alan Bond may have little time for reading as he struggles to preserve and maintain the splendid 1929 London General AEC Regal, T31. Also in the London area, Philip Wallis looks at the independent operators that were allowed to run buses in the London Transport area.

Where on earth would you find ex-London RTs and an RTL in service alongside Daimler Fleetlines and classic US buses? The US buses provide the clue; ex-pat Michael Dryhurst describes the fascinating fleet run by the Association of Students at the University of California, Davis (ASUCD), better known as Unitrans.

The doyen of road transport journalists, Alan Townsin, examines the often-overlooked topic of early small diesel buses, and Steve Lockwood tells the story of a unique batch of trolleybuses that ran for three different English municipal fleets.

There are photographic contributions from Reg Wilson, on South Wales company buses, and the distinguished photographers who make up Fotobus contribute some of their earlier work. R. D. Okill visited the Isle of Wight with his camera in 1938, and Cornwall in the early postwar years, and we show some of the resulting photos.

This year we have included a number of the most popular regular items from the bi-monthly magazine *Classic Bus*. There are four Checkpoint columns in the book, instant information on widely varied topics. And Alan Millar proves that not all buses were Blunderbuses with Classic Wonderbus, a variation on his regular column. One of the notorious Geoffs – Burrows of that ilk – provides more answers to readers' questions in Q&A, and cracks the Albion chassis designations in CCC.

Transport journalist John Aldridge provides a regular column in the magazine on significant events he attended, and in I Was There he recalls a routine event, the opening of a new bus garage.

There is a painting by G. S. Cooper, and the Open Platform has been given over to Stephen Morris, editor of the monthly magazine *Buses*.

If you are not already a *Classic Bus* magazine reader, and this book has given you a taste of the nostalgia it contains – look out for it on the news-stands. In the magazine, as in this Yearbook, we aim to give readers the best bus writing and photography around.

**Gavin Booth**
Edinburgh

---

Front Cover: The cover photos, from the camera of the renowned bus photographer Peter Durham, who retired from bus photography during 1997, show three of the more popular types of bus in preservation in the UK today. The cover photo shows ex-Cheltenham District No 1003, a 1967 Bristol RELL6L with Eastern Coach Works 44-seat dual-door body. It has been restored to its original livery by the Cheltenham Bus Preservation Group, and we are grateful to secretary, Mike Hilltout, for arranging this road run on its old route, 587 from Cheltenham to Cleeve Hill. Peter Durham

Page 1: Edinburgh Corporation became an enthusiastic convert to the Leyland Titan double-deck chassis in the 1950s, as recounted in the article beginning on page 42. The most famous — perhaps notorious — of the Edinburgh Titans were the 300 bought in 1954-7 with ultra-lightweight Metro-Cammell Orion bodywork, and one of the first buses into service in 1954 is seen on a tram replacement service on the city's most famous thoroughfare, Princes Street.

Back Cover: Two more popular types among preservationists. The Leyland Titan PD2 competed with other models, mainly from AEC, Daimler and Guy, for municipal business in the 1950s and 1960s. This Glasgow Corporation PD2/24 model (above), with fully-automatic gearbox, has Alexander bodywork, and is seen at the Scottish Vintage Bus Museum at Lathalmond, Fife. Below is a Bedford OB with Duple Vista 29-seat body, a combination that is well represented in the preservation ranks. This 1950 example was new to Gittins of Oswestry, and passed via Mid Wales Motorways into preservation with Meredith's Coaches of Malpas, Cheshire. It is seen leaving Meredith's garage driven by Ray Jones. We are grateful to Ray, and to Kevin and Ben Meredith for arranging this special road run. Peter Durham

# VICTORIA

## in the 1950s

### MICHAEL H. C. BAKER remembers Victoria Coach Station at a time when the shape of coaches was changing dramatically

*Victoria line-up in November 1954, with (left to right) newly-delivered North Western Burlingham Seagull-bodied Leyland Tiger Cub PSUCI/2T No 565, and two Bristol LS with ECW bodies – United LS6B No BUT9, also new, and Royal Blue 1953 LS6G No 1295.*

All photos by Michael H. C. Baker except where otherwise credited

I HAVE TO ADMIT that living within eight miles of the heart of London conferred on one a distinct sense of superiority for, like it or not, there was more variety in the transport scene here than anywhere else in the land. How else could it be in a capital city? Fortunately before I could become totally insufferable I started to travel and rapidly became aware that the rest of the country was not without its attractions, indeed some bits were quite exotic. However, this did not diminish the appeal of London and whenever pocket money and indulgent visiting aunts and uncles could be prevailed upon I took myself – and them, sometimes – off up to one of the main line termini or a strategic spot where the maximum number of buses, trams, trolleys and Green Line coaches could be observed going about their business. My usual terminus was Victoria; years later I was to work there during college holidays as a porter. Just down the road was as good a place as one could imagine for observing long distance coaches, Victoria Coach Station. I didn't enjoy carting bulging suitcases on humid August afternoons from one to the other, but no such possible exertions clouded my horizons over 40 years ago when the accompanying pictures were taken.

The mid-1950s was an especially interesting period

in British coaching history, for the underfloor engine era had begun in 1950 – 1948 if you lived in Midland Red territory, for in the early postwar years that unique company was ahead of the field. By 1955 the Leyland Royal Tiger and Tiger Cub, the AEC Regal Mk IV and Reliance, and the Bristol LS were well established (one also met underfloor Dennises and Guys as well) and were the frontline troops in most of the big company fleets which ran in and out of Victoria. With their bold, full-fronted appearance and high floor and roof line they looked vastly superior to their halfcab predecessors. Most fleet managers tried to keep these latter allegedly antique-looking veterans well out of sight, even though the newest were scarcely five years old. Others, in a futile attempt at modernisation, were rebuilt with full fronts which more often than not had the opposite effect to that desired. Come summer weekends then anything which could turn a wheel was pressed into service. Not only

did the last generation of Leyland PS1 Tigers, AEC Mk I and III Regals and Bristol L-types reappear in force, but there were still plenty of their prewar counterparts around. Although petrol rationing ended in 1950 the demand for coach travel continued to increase and when every proper member of the coach fleet was out on the road on a sunny bank holiday Saturday or Monday, humble single-deck buses and even the occasional double-decker, were drafted in and sent up to the capital. Whilst passengers had every right to consider themselves pretty unlucky to spend several hours in a conveyance ill-equipped for such a lengthy journey – although the view from the top deck of a double-decker was considerable compensation – if it was that or nothing then you suffered in silence and made the best of it.

**Pressed into service**

Opposite the coach station owned by London Coastal Coaches, a consortium of all the leading coach companies, was the headquarters of British Overseas Airways Corporation where one could board a deep

Top: *Maidstone & District No CO32 parked in a side street near Victoria Coach Station on Easter Saturday 1955. It is an AEC Regal I with 32-seat Beadle body built in 1948 and withdrawn in 1959. There is something very satisfying about a coach like this in its immaculate off-white and deep green livery. The E5 was the Faversham service.*

Above: *Looking like a prewar coach, Maidstone & District No CO556 had a 1937 Leyland Tiger TS7 chassis, but a 1949 Harrington body. Seen at Victoria in April 1955 when Benny Hill was starring at the Prince of Wales theatre, No CO556 was sold in 1958, but similar DKT, No 16 survives in preservation.*

blue and white BOAC coach for Heathrow Airport. Coaches from across the road were sometimes pressed into airline service whilst awaiting their return journey home. The BOAC building was an impressive white concrete edifice, the back of which stared down at my train as it pulled into Victoria station. The London Coastal Coaches headquarters was even more imposing, a fine example of 1930s art deco. One of the adjoining bridges, Eccleston Bridge, was the hub of the Green Line network, whilst down the road, outside the railway station, was the London Transport red bus terminus. So all in all there was no finer place to observe psvs going about their business.

Honesty compels one to admit that, excellent as the Green Line 10T10s, TFs, Qs and their RF successors were, they were by no stretch of the imagination true long-distances coaches of the sort which patronised the establishment down the road. The only real coaches London Transport owned at this time were the RFWs, AEC Mk IV Regals dating from 1951, fitted with specially-built ECW bodies, not at all like anything else which came out of Lowestoft at this time, other than a batch of identical ones for Festival of Britain work with Tillings Travel. The RFWs could occasionally be seen in Victoria Coach Station, whence they worked tours, but were more often found laying over at the bus station.

Victoria Coach Station could hardly have had a more impressive address, Buckingham Palace Road no less, at the opposite end of the street from the Queen's bijou residence. The original coach station had

Left: *East Kent coaches were a familiar sight at Victoria. JG 5422 is a Leyland Tiger TS7 of 1935 with 32-seat Park Royal body, seen in June 1955 and sold five months later.*

Below: *Representing the more modern East Kent fleet of the time, FFN 449 at Battersea Park in May 1956. It was one of East Kent's original underfloor-engined coaches, a 1951 Leyland Royal Tiger with Park Royal centre entrance body. The coach ferried passengers from Victoria to Lympne, where they flew Silver City Airways to Beauvais, and then on by coach to Paris.*

opened in 1928, at Lupus Street, Pimlico, and was no more than an expanse of empty ground with space for 150 vehicles, fronted by a Victorian villa converted to offices. In 1932 London Coastal Coaches moved north-westwards into up-market Belgravia when the present coach station opened on the corner of Buckingham Palace Road and Elizabeth Street. At peak times, despite there being an overflow establishment across Elizabeth Street, the station could barely cope with all

Top: *This handsome Southdown coach, seen parked in a square near Eccleston Bridge in June 1955, is a 1936 Leyland Tiger TS7 with 32-seat Burlingham coach body. It was waiting to work a relief to Portsmouth.*

Above: *Southdown's first batch of postwar coaches were 1947-built Leyland Tiger PS1/1 with ECW 31-seat bodies. No 1243 is seen at Battersea in August 1954; that winter it was converted to a bus and reseated.*

There were only six of these Windover-bodied Leyland Tiger PS1s in the Southdown fleet, built in 1947 and the only Windover-bodied coaches ever owned by the company. No 1273 is seen in Victoria in April 1955.

Representing the brief interest in full-fronted coaches on front-engined chassis, Southdown No 1312, a Leyland Tiger PS1 of 1947 with a Duple 32-seat body rebuilt to this style in 1954, parked in a street near Victoria Coach Station in June 1955.

the comings and goings. There was little room for coaches which had arrived earlier in the day to lay up whilst awaiting their afternoon or evening return, and whilst many managed to find accommodation in the railway yard on the south side of the Thames at Battersea beside the approach to Grosvenor Bridge and opposite the famous power station, others parked wherever they could. Thus a stroll around the elegant squares of Pimlico and Belgravia would often bring its

reward, although what the residents thought of having a Southdown Tiger or Maidstone & District Regal, however handsome we cognoscenti considered them, blocking their view for several hours seems to have gone unrecorded.

**Bodywork requirements**

Companies as large as these two south coast giants, and Ribble, Black & White, United, etc, could afford

Top: *A rarity in the Southdown fleet, one of the two Bedford OB/Duple Vista 27-seat coaches bought in 1948 for the Hayling Island service. No 71 is seen in June 1955.*

Above: *From East Anglia, Eastern National No 300, a 1948 Bristol L5G with 31-seat dual-purpose ECW body, at Victoria in April 1955.*

Top: *A Relief Car for Plymouth, Royal Blue 1951 Bristol LL6B with Duple body, No 1256, at Victoria around 1956.*
Michael H. C. Baker collection

Above: *The only 'proper' coaches in the London Transport fleet were the RFW class, AEC Regal IV with unusual ECW bodies. RFW5 is seen outside Victoria railway station in August 1961.*

*Midland Red S10 bus No 3647 caught at Victoria on Easter Saturday 1955, after unloading 44 not altogether satisfied customers from Leicester.*

to stipulate their own bodywork requirements and many of their coaches were instantly recognisable, not only by their livery, but by their design. This had been particularly true in the years immediately before World War 2, but in the immediate postwar period this became less so, not least because there were more customers than suppliers, and operators were happy to get their hands on anything at all in order to catch up with the years of neglect and deprivation. Some prewar coaches were rebodied, others were refurbished, whilst some concerns largely made do with what they had got whilst they waited for the new generation of underfloor vehicles to come on stream.

There were probably more Duple-bodied vehicles to be seen than any other type. The Hendon-based firm tended to set the style which everyone else followed, certainly in the period immediately before the underfloor-engined coaches came in. Always associated with Bedford, which was a chassis supplier largely ignored by the big operators and thus not a common sight at Victoria at this time, the one exception was the OB. This classic design was the last of normal-control layout in production in the UK on any scale, its only rival, and not a serious one, being Commer. I once embarked on a school outing to

Cambridge, organised by our music master, in a Duple-bodied Commer. We enjoyed ourselves but the trip was not an unqualified success for everyone, the master falling into the Cam whilst attempting to re-live his undergraduate days, and the Commer broke down just as we were leaving. From a schoolboy's point of view a teacher falling into the water would make any trip successful beyond his wildest dreams, and no-one much minded getting home late. I recall the driver getting quite shirty when one of us attempted to take a photograph of him fiddling about in the innards of his machine, the bonnet up, motor car style.

Around this time Commers suddenly became quite popular with some of the big boys, a number of them buying the integral Beadle with Commer running units. In the early 1960s I helped drive a Plaxton-bodied version overland to Afghanistan, or rather that is as far as the Iranian desert where it expired, but that's another story.

The Duple-bodied Bedford OB was so popular that a number of companies which normally dealt only in Leylands, AECs, Bristols and the like, found a place for a few in their fleets; Crosville, Southdown, East Kent and Western National spring to mind. Plaxton, on the other hand, had as yet only got a toehold in the market. Duple's chief rivals were Harrington of Hove, Burlingham of Blackpool – and ECW whose designs were confined to state-owned companies which meant, almost inevitably, they were built on the Bristol LS, producing a classic combination. British-built chassis and bodywork had a total monopoly, the closest Victoria got to a foreign product being the Wagon Lits sleeping cars on the Night Ferry from Paris and Brussels.

Just as the introduction of the underfloor engine immediately rendered the halfcab out of date, so the opening of the first motorway, the Preston bypass section of the M6 in 1958, would lead to a new generation of coaches. Despite this, some of those at work in the mid-1950s would have very long lives lasting into the preservation era and thus are still with us. **CB**

*Michael Baker is a schoolteacher and has written some 25 books on transport and places, as well as many articles.*

# CHECKPOINT

## No1: Crosville Motor Services

**Born:** Chester 1905 as Crosville Motor Company.
**Parents:** G. Crosland-Taylor and Georges Ville.
**Their objective:** Ville was a car manufacturer of sorts, with premises in Paris. Crosland-Taylor planned to assemble and market Ville's cars under a combination of their surnames. He only built five, dashing any hopes of turning Chester into one of the centres of the fledgling British motor industry.
**What happened next?:** By 1910, thoughts were turning to running buses and two – presumably secondhand – vehicles, a Herald and a Belgian-built Germain, were bought but never run. By the following year, Crosland-Taylor had found something more suitable in the shape of an Albion and he started running from Chester to the fast-growing town of Ellesmere Port, providing a direct alternative to a convoluted journey by train. By the outbreak of World War 1, the fleet was creeping into double figures, new Daimlers and Letchworth-built Lacres were being bought and a second front was opened up with routes radiating out of Crewe.
**Did Crosville have a good war?:** Indubitably. A munitions factory at Queensferry helped it expand into North Wales, providing the basis for postwar growth, part of which was undertaken with ex-War Department Crossleys. This also helped foster further expansion into Merseyside where another sort of war was averted by reaching agreement with Birkenhead Corporation to let its buses run beyond its boundaries in return for Crosville gaining access to the ferry pier at Woodside and lucrative traffic flows to Liverpool. By July 1929, Crosville had 322 buses across northwest England and northern Wales.
**An auspicious date?:** Yes. That was when the company was bought outright by the London, Midland & Scottish Railway, which had inherited North Wales feeder bus routes run by the London & North Western Railway since 1905. Crosville's grey livery was replaced by LMS's maroon, the fleetname became LMS (Crosville), acquisitions of North Wales operators added another 127 vehicles to the fleet and 118 new Leylands – popular purchases since 1921 – were bought for fleet renewal.
**And a settled pattern evolved?:** Hardly. These were times of rapid change and turmoil for the bus industry. The Tilling & British Automobile Traction combine had been formed in 1928 and, in May 1930, TBAT bought control of Crosville and changed the name to Crosville Motor Services. By 1935, further consolidation and expansion had taken Crosville into Runcorn, with around 60 acquisitions along the way including the memorably-named Zacchaeus Woodfin of Tarvin, Cheshire. Ribble's Liverpool-London express was added in 1931.
**Were there other initial changes?:** In 1935, alphanumerical fleetnumbering was introduced. This was further refined in 1958 into a fondly-remembered (and still used by PMT) system of three prefix letters denoting vehicle type, chassis type and engine make (eg SLB290 for a 1952 Bristol LWL6B with bus seats). A prefixed route numbering system followed in later years, with regional groupings from A to S, plus X for express services.
**And how good was its second war?:** It brought more expansion to meet the needs of armaments production in Wrexham, Chester and Crewe which, alone, needed over 300 dedicated buses. Airfields and army camps generated their own requirements and the company coped with other hazards of war, like air raids and shortages of parts, vehicles and staff. War also saw another change of ownership in 1942, with Tilling & BAT breaking up, Crosville passing to Tilling and changing its livery to green in 1944. This led, in turn, to a change of purchasing policy, with Leylands forsaken and utility Bristol K6As coming towards the end of the war and paving the way for newer Bristols that followed. The fleet had grown to 1,300. Unable to invest in as many buses as normal, Tilling's had instructed Crosville to invest in property instead.
**Were tears shed on nationalisation?:** Not if the title of general manager W. J. Crosland-Taylor's 1953 book, *State Owned Without Tears*, is to be believed. Acquisition by the British Transport Commission in 1948 was followed by much-needed investment in new vehicles, but by the early-1950s this younger Crosland-Taylor was worrying about the miles of unremunerative services in Wales, wondering whether the company would have been wiser sticking to Merseyside and leaving Wales to independents, and wishing the industry could cut its costs by being allowed to run higher capacity one-man buses on country routes. In 1964, it bought two Commer minibuses for routes in mid-Wales.
**But Crosville survived?:** Yes, but by 1970 when National Bus was in charge, it took speedy action to begin axeing rural routes and seeking subsidies for their survival. Even so, NBC fostered further expansion in 1972 by transferring North Western's Cheshire routes into Crosville and shunting bits of South Wales and Western Welsh on to its southern end, along with all sorts of AECs, Leylands and Dennises hitherto unknown in a largely Bristol fleet.
**Are you sure that was all?:** Are you to be excused the appalling pun? Yes, there also were 100 Seddon RUs bought to bridge the gap between shortages of Bristol RELLs and delivery of Leyland Nationals.
**And were tears shed on privatisation?:** If they weren't, they should have been. The government compelled NBC to split Crosville in two in 1986. Its subsequent fate falls beyond the scope of this book, but suffice to say that by the time you read this, the name will be confined to buses run in Chester and the Wirral. And they are neither green, maroon nor grey. **ALM**

*Classic Crosville, and a classic Tony Moyes portrait of Bristol LL6B No SLB276 at Dawn, near Colwyn Bay, in August 1964.*
A. Moyes

# TWO DOORS FOR LEEDS

## Like several of Britain's larger municipalities, in the 1960s and 1970s Leeds turned to two-door double-deckers. J. B. PARKIN tells the story

THE INTRODUCTION of rear-engined chassis to the streets of Leeds by its transport department was not carried out with any great enthusiasm as was the case with many other operators who immediately ordered large quantities of firstly Leyland Atlanteans and subsequently other chassis makes as these came on to the market. Initially, a batch of 10 each of Daimler Fleetlines and Leyland Atlanteans came out in 1964 and 1965 respectively, being followed by a further 15 of each type delivered in 1966/7. These were the only 30ft-long buses of these types purchased, traditional rear platform double-deckers being purchased in the main up to 1966. It was with the introduction of the 10-metre chassis length, nominally 33ft, that things began to change with the forthcoming one-person operation boom.

*Leeds had operated two-door buses before the 1968 Fleetlines. This 1962 AEC Reliance 470 had a Roe 41-seat two-door body, and is seen arriving at London's Earls Court, where it was an exhibit at the 1962 Commercial Motor Show. It was one of five similar buses bought for driver-only services.*

It was at the 1966 Commercial Motor Show, held at Earls Court, London, between 23 September and 1 October that the first longer Fleetline for Leeds appeared, this being No 131 with Roe body, being followed by a production batch of 14 others, Nos 132-45, in 1967. A batch of 30 Leyland Atlanteans bodied by Park Royal to an almost identical design followed in September 1968. All these buses were built to a most

attractive design of Roe body, with large panoramic side windows, but fitted with a front entrance/exit only. It was thought in Leeds that a dual doorway design would be more suitable for one-person operation and with a new general manager in Thomas Lord, a new style body was evolved with the coachbuilders, Charles H. Roe Ltd. This became known as the Leeds standard body and remained so for all remaining deliveries to the transport department, creating a design unique to the city. In all, a total of 295 were built for Leeds, these consisting of 85 Fleetlines and 210 Atlanteans, along with a small number for other operators to be described later. Seating on all batches was 45 upstairs and 33 in the lower deck.

September 1968 saw the first examples appearing from the Roe factory, the first to appear in public from a batch of 15 numbered 146-60 were again at an Earls Court Commercial Motor Show between the 20th and

*Leeds No 131 appeared at the 1966 Commercial Show, a 33ft long Daimler Fleetline with Roe 78-seat bodywork, but with a single doorway. The panoramic side windows and frontal styling owe something to Alexander bodies built for Edinburgh Corporation.*

28th of that month. No 156 was displayed on the Daimler stand and No 158 on the Roe stand. Both were from the final five of the batch, fitted with the then new Gardner 6LXB 10.45-litre engine and Daimatic fully-automatic transmission with power-assisted steering. By contrast, the first 10, Nos 146-55, did not have power steering and were powered by the smaller Gardner 6LX engine with semi-automatic gearboxes. All had 8ft 2½in wide Roe bodies with panoramic side windows, the design having a slight peaked effect at both front and rear. The livery was altered to a new style, using the former dark and light

green colours in the reversed positions, giving a mainly light green bus with dark green roof, cantrail, lower saloon window surrounds and with a broad band below those windows on which was positioned a new-style insignia by the entrance on the nearside and in a forward position on the offside. New-style reflective registration plates were fitted and another new feature was the advertisement spaces bounded by a metal strip with radiused corners. As well as the usual front destination displays, a side route number and terminal point was positioned on the nearside near the entrance. Electro-pneumatically-operated jack-knife doors were fitted, with an interlock device on the centre exit doors preventing them opening whilst the vehicle was in motion.

**High standard**

Shortwave radio equipment was fitted plus public address facilities in each saloon. As the buses were intended for one-man operation (as it then was) in Leeds, a periscope was fitted along with a passenger counting device for the upper saloon. The Roe safety staircase with two square landings and no curved stairs was forward-ascending, with luggage space and conductor's locker underneath. All in all, these buses were finished to the usual high standard which had by the mid-1960s become normal on Leeds buses, with extensive use of Formica panelling and comfortable deep seating, all forward-facing in the upper saloon in a green leathercloth. The lower deck seats were more

*An official view of Leeds No 388, a 1970 Leyland Atlantean PDR2/1 with the style of Roe bodywork that was to become familiar on the two-door buses bought between 1968 and 1974. The rather drab two-tone green livery was used to denote one-person-operated buses.*

unusual: these were finished in a green and white material, the rear having a seat for five passengers whilst the next pair of seats on each side faced the rear, being fitted over the wheelarches. There were then four pairs of seats on the offside before the staircase, while on the nearside there were three pairs of seats before the centre exit doors, followed by a further two pairs, all forward-facing. At the front of the saloon on either side were seats for three, facing inwards. British Leyland plaques were fitted for the Earls Court display, but these were removed prior to entering passenger use.

Before entering service, another of the final five buses made a journey to Lille in France, when No 159 departed on Tuesday, 8 October, in connection with a British Shopping Week held there. Lille is a twin city to Leeds. For its journey, it too was fitted with radio equipment similar to Nos 156 and 158.

With one exception, No 155 which entered service on the 6 December, the whole batch entered service from Middleton garage on 24 November 1968, conductor-operated on the Middleton/Dewsbury

*Leyland Atlantean No 413 at Corn Exchange, Leeds, in the later simplified version of the West Yorkshire PTE livery.*
H Heyworth

Road/Roundhay circular routes 2, 3, 10, 12 and 18-21 inclusive. It has already been mentioned that three of the batch were fitted with radio equipment – this was fitted to the remaining 12 buses from May 1969, in preparation for the introduction of double-deck one-man operation on service 49 (Hyde Park to Old Farnley) from 13 July, for which purpose Nos 153-60 were transferred from Middleton to Bramley garage. The remainder followed to Bramley in October 1969. Subsequently, new batches of buses were delivered already fitted with radio, for which an extensive control room was eventually fitted up at Swinegate head office.

A further batch of 40 Fleetlines with the CRG6LXB chassis appeared in September and October 1969 (Nos 161-80) and between March and May 1970 (Nos 181-200). The passenger counter display for the upper saloon had not been a success where it was originally positioned and the new series and all succeeding batches had it moved to a position below the staircase mirror, where passengers ascending the stairs could read how many seats remained unoccupied. For a few days only on entering service, 161-80 started work from Torre Road garage, but from 12 October 1969, Nos 161-72 went on to Seacroft garage and Nos 173-80 to Sovereign Street. This garage also received Nos 181-7

when new, with Nos 188-95 going to Headingley and Nos 196-200 to Torre Road.

**Long Atlanteans**

These were the last Gardner-engined Fleetlines purchased, but by this time, delivery had commenced of Leyland Atlanteans of similar dimensions, Nos 386-405 designated type PDR2/1 being the first series received, with 401-5 being the first in the fleet with spring brakes in place of the normal handbrakes (a feature fitted to all subsequent Atlanteans). With identical bodies to those fitted to Fleetlines, these buses entered service in January and February 1970, being allocated to Bramley garage, displacing Fleetlines Nos 146-60 to Seacroft garage. The next 20 buses, Nos 406-25, all came out in July 1970, differing from the previous batch in having fully-automatic gearboxes. They were all allocated to Middleton garage.

Deliveries now came thick and fast, with No 426 upwards differing slightly in that the side destination

On the first day of West Yorkshire PTE operations, 1 April 1974, Leyland Atlantean No 447 is on display at Garforth wearing the original Verona green/buttermilk 'candy stripe' livery.
J. B. Parkin

indicator was omitted and a large number aperture placed in the front nearside window. Nos 426-65 all entered service between September 1970 and March 1971, No 428 again being an exhibit at an Earls Court Show, held between 18-26 September 1970, being displayed on the Roe stand. It differed in minor points from the remainder, in that it did not have mudguards, but just a cutaway panel of squarish appearance. Continuous strip lighting was installed, along with a new type of passenger counter for the top deck; electrically-operated indicator box glass and a modified heating and ventilation system. All of Nos 426-65 were initially allocated to Sovereign Street garage, with the first three moving to Middleton in May 1972 and the remainder gradually migrating to Bramley garage over a period.

The final batch of PDR2/1 buses entered service in September and October 1971, being Nos 466-95. Again similar to earlier deliveries, they had larger extractors fitted for the upper saloon ventilation system. The first few entered service from Sovereign Street garage, but all were at Bramley by October 1971. Up to and including this batch, all bodies had been fitted with a public address system. This was seldom used in Leeds and from November 1971 the equipment started to be removed from buses, the speaker apertures being panelled over with Formica.

With all these new deliveries, the introduction of further one-man operation began to increase pace, with the conversion first of relatively quiet routes until soon cross-city services were tackled, with the intention being to have all services so operated. In due course this did happen, although not until after the formation of the West Yorkshire PTE.

### Leyland engines

Mention should next be made of a series of 30 Daimler Fleetlines, these being fitted with Leyland engines being designated type CRL6-33. Initially numbered 751-80, it had been planned to number these buses 201-30 after the Gardner-engined Fleetlines, but a late decision after they had been registered JUM 201-30L caused them to become 751 upwards in a completely separate series. They did, however, become Nos 201-30 in March 1974, very shortly before the PTE took effect. Entry into service was between September 1972 and January 1973. No 761 had been another Commercial Motor Show exhibit, keeping up the Leeds tradition at Earls Court, between 22-30 September 1972. Its body varied from the remainder of

the series by having opening front ventilator windows fitted in the front bulkhead, along with other additional ventilation louvres. A blower unit was situated by each door, so that when opened a curtain of hot air was blown through apertures above the doorways. (A feature which did not last long in use!) A new design of material was used for lower saloon seating, this being of a yellow diamond design, while upper saloon seating was in a pale olive vinyl material. Carpet was fitted in the lower saloon. All the series were fitted with Sundym panoramic windows on either side of the upper saloon, in order to cut down glare from the sun, as many complaints were made when the design was new with its forced ventilation and lack of opening windows. The front and rear side windows remained fitted with normal clear glass, so that when viewed from the side, the difference between the Sundym and clear windows could be noticed. Slightly earlier in July 1972, Leyland Atlanteans Nos 399 and 431 had been experimentally fitted with this glass. Initially operated from Sovereign Street garage, Nos 751-80 all soon moved to Torre Road, where they were established by early 1973.

Delivery then commenced again of Leyland Atlanteans with the standard bodies and later modifications, but the chassis of all future deliveries was of the newly-introduced AN68/2R type. Nos 496-515 came out in January and February 1973, these being quickly followed by 516-30 in April and May, the latter differing in that they were fitted with front opening ventilators to the upper saloon bulkhead windows, as on Fleetline 761. These were also fitted to all subsequent deliveries up to No 595. All of Nos 496-530 were initially allocated to Sovereign Street garage.

Soon after, in September and October 1973, a

further order appeared, numbered 531-55. Again allocated initially to Sovereign Street, Nos 531-50 quickly moved to Headingley garage and Nos 551-555 to Middleton, which garage also received the final order, Nos 556-95. These commenced delivery in December 1973 and continued until the last entered service on 7 June 1974, this being No 581.

### Last for Leeds

The West Yorkshire PTE had commenced operations on 1 April 1974, taking over all vehicles and services of Leeds City Transport and Nos 581/6-90/92-5 were all delivered new to the PTE in its livery of Verona green and buttermilk. Additionally, Nos 576/8/83/90 were delivered new to the PTE, but were received in Leeds colours. The very last bus to be delivered to the Leeds Transport Department was No 591 on 29 March 1974, coming into use on the very same day as it was delivered. This was a most unusual event, as new buses generally were well checked over by the Engineering Section before being released to passenger use. Thus came an end to deliveries of this Leeds standard body, as all future double deck deliveries to the PTE, including buses ordered by Leeds before PTE formation date and not then delivered were to be of front entrance design only, reverting to 30ft length.

It should be mentioned at this point that three buses of the standard Leeds dual-door design were actually built new for small operators. These were built by Roe

when a small operator placed a tiny order, ie one or two buses, when construction was done alongside an order for a larger quantity. The three buses built in this category were all on Leyland Atlantean chassis, the first to be built being delivered in July 1971. This was the well-known GUP 6H purchased by Weardale Motor Services. This was followed by OCS 345L, delivered in May 1973 to T. & E. Docherty of A1 Service, Ardrossan. The final bus of this trio had quite a history before entering passenger service. It was ordered by Green Bus of Rugeley, but the order was cancelled when the operator was taken over by Midland Red. Being in build, it was completed and then sold to Colin S. Pegg of Caston and given the registration number RVF 564M. It did not enter service before August 1974 and it was therefore re-registered to SPW 92N before coming into use and earning the distinction of being the last of its design to appear.

Also built for airport work to the same general design, but featuring only a single front entrance and with large luggage compartments were two small batches of Leyland Atlanteans, these being GML 846-51J for BOAC (as it then was) and LLH 5-9K for Halls Coaches of Hounslow. These had originally been constructed as CJH 611-5X, but were re-registered prior to use. Delivered in February 1972; LLH 5, 6 and 8K were painted in TWA livery and the other two in Valliant Silverline colours.

All of the Leeds 33ft buses passed to the West

Yorkshire PTE, but by launch day on 1 April 1974, Atlantean No 447 had been one of several buses painted into experimental liveries. Initially in a mid-green and buttermilk, the shade was changed to verona green in March 1974, No 485 also being similarly treated. No 447 was duly displayed on inaugural day at a press conference held at the Mercury Motor Inn, Garforth Bridge, along with buses of several other types and representing all new districts of the PTE. Eventually, all the 33ft buses were painted into the new colours.

## Modifications

Over the years, various minor modifications were made to buses, such as the fitting of cowls which protruded over the ventilator intakes above the front windows and the removal of air scoops at either side of the front near the destination indicators. Some of the buses with upper saloon front opening windows from 516 upwards had them removed and replaced by fixed panes of glass, as the original type were working loose and proving extremely draughty, but on the whole very few changes was made to the buses, many of which had lengthy lives.

*Leyland Atlantean No 563 in Vicar Lane. This was one of the final 40 buses of the dual doorway type for Leeds City Transport, and is seen in early West Yorkshire PTE livery.*
H. Heyworth

The first to be withdrawn was Daimler Fleetline No 167, badly damaged by fire working to Elland Road on a Leeds United football special on 15 September 1979. Normal withdrawals commenced in 1980 with both Fleetlines and Atlanteans, with the former being withdrawn the soonest. All the Gardner-engined Fleetlines had gone by June 1984, with the newest of this manufacture, those with Leyland engines, going between 1984 and 1985. By deregulation in October 1986, inroads were being made into the Atlanteans, but a total of 120, of which Nos 434 and 465 were the oldest, passed to Yorkshire Rider Ltd on its formation. Many of these were repainted in its colours, yet another variation of green with jonquil relief. All the PDR2/1 buses had been withdrawn by January 1989, but many of the AN68/2R breed outlasted later single doorway Atlanteans delivered to the PTE, with the last examples, Nos 580/7/9/90 running to 31 March 1993. New regulations on additional interlocking safety features on the centre exit doors came into force the following day, causing the final withdrawal of the type in Leeds. No 580 was the last of the survivors to run in service, operating out of Bramley garage on service 10 from Middleton to Corn Exchange. The other three had spent their final days working from Torre Road garage, these coming from the few delivered new to

the PTE. No 580 was a genuine Leeds City Transport bus and not only did it have the distinction of being the final example of its type in passenger use, it was the last Leeds bus and also the last one from any of the constituents of the PTE.

Several Atlanteans had been transferred to the training fleet, but the last of these, No 9376, formerly No 555, was withdrawn on 12 July 1993.

By far the majority of both Fleetlines and Atlanteans passed after withdrawal to breakers in the Barnsley area, but odd ones did escape and found further use with other operators. Space does not allow us to list these, but notable disposals were of Atlanteans Nos 401-4 by the PTE to Ipswich Transport as Nos 41-4, and of No 471 to National Express Ltd, for whom Yorkshire Rider converted it to a shuttle lounge for use in Victoria Coach Station, London; surely a most unusual use for a former Leeds bus! Several others were converted to exhibition vehicles, for which their length and dual-door layout made them particularly suitable. More recently, Nos 561 and 595 were rebodied with East Lancs single-deck bus bodies for Hylton Castle, East Boldon, near Sunderland, where re-registered they looked just like new buses. They have subsequently been sold to another operator.

Yet another era has ceased with the withdrawal of these fine buses, built on two different chassis, both of which gave extremely good service over many years. For service use, Leyland Atlantean 511 claims the record, serving the City of Leeds under three owners for two months short of 20 years, truly an excellent record for another classic bus type. **CB**

*Brian Parkin worked for many years in the coaching industry, retiring from the position of northeast area operations manager for National Express. He has always been interested in transport, both road and rail, taking particular interest in local services. He is hon editor of the* West Yorkshire Metro Transport News *which covers local operations in that area.*

## SUMMARY OF BATCHES OF LEEDS DUAL-DOOR DOUBLE-DECKERS*

| Fleet Nos | Registrations | Type | Built |
|---|---|---|---|
| 146-55 | PUB 146-55G | Daimler Fleetline CRG6LX | 1968 |
| 156-60 | PUB 156-60G | Daimler Fleetline CRG6LXB | 1968 |
| 161-200 | UNW 161-200H | Daimler Fleetline CRG6LXB | 1969-70 |
| 386-425 | UNW 386-425H | Leyland Atlantean PDR2/1 | 1970 |
| 426-45 | XUM 426-45J | Leyland Atlantean PDR2/1 | 1970/1 |
| 446-65 | ANW 446-65J | Leyland Atlantean PDR2/1 | 1971 |
| 466-95 | DUA 466-95K | Leyland Atlantean PDR2/1 | 1971 |
| 496-530 | JUG 496-530L | Leyland Atlantean AN68/2R | 1973 |
| 751-80+ | JUM 201-30L | Daimler Fleetline CRL6-33 | 1972-3 |
| 531-55 | PUM 531-55M | Leyland Atlantean AN68/2R | 1973 |
| 556-95 | SUG 556-95M | Leyland Atlantean AN68/2R | 1973-4 |

*All fitted with Roe H45/33D bodies.
+ Renumbered 201-30 in March 1974.

*Still in full Leeds livery, Atlantean No 545 in New York Street, Leeds, in August 1976.*
J. B. Parkin

# CLASSIC WONDER BUS

In spite of its title, not all buses covered in the magazine *Classic Bus* are actually classics. Some are far from it, and in each issue ALAN MILLAR nominates a Classic Blunderbus, a model that proved to be a real lemon. As an antidote to this, in the Yearbook Alan offers us a model that was, by any measure, an undoubted success

FOR THOSE OF YOU who believe that classic buses ceased to be classic the day designers swapped the positions of engines and platforms, I apologise now, for I fear this year's nomination for a wonderbus will offend your sense of decency. But why am I apologising? A bus which saved its manufacturer from otherwise likely demise and went on to secure nearly 12,000 sales at home and abroad must have had a lot going for it, even if most had doors at the front and all had engines firmly in the back.

I'm talking of a bus which outsold the mass-produced Leyland National by a margin of 50%, the RT in all its forms – AEC and Leyland, narrow and wide, prewar and postwar, London Transport and provincial customers – by a margin of over 60% and which, over 20 years, achieved 65% of the sales clocked up by all four produced marks of the AEC Regent in almost twice that time. My nomination for the antidote to *Classic Bus*'s Blunderbus award is the Daimler (later Leyland) Fleetline.

Yes, I hear you scream letters like 'D', 'M' and 'S' and words like single-decker. Neither London Transport's experience with and treatment of the Fleetline nor the lengthening of the model into a 36ft standee saloon did it any favours, but as I hope *CB* readers will realise when those models are reached in the magazine's series of Blunderbus articles, they are insufficient grounds to damn the Fleetline as a bad bus. On the contrary, I believe it was a truly wonderful bus for its time.

## Familiarity and satisfaction
Before considering the features of the model, just recall Daimler's own position in the market. As one of the few manufacturers of wartime double-deckers, it took advantage of customers' familiarity and

satisfaction with its products to cash in on the immediate postwar boom. Indeed it was so successful that by 1948 the national press was cheerfully recycling a rumour – denied strongly by Daimler – that the company was going to pull out of the luxury car market and concentrate on buses.

Yet by 1957, when the flamboyant, not to say controversial chairman and managing director Sir Bernard Docker and the far-from-publicity-shy Lady Docker were being ousted from the board of parent company BSA, Daimler's grip on the bus market was slipping fast. While disproportionate management effort had gone into ventures like the Dockers' gold, silver and other exotic cars, sales of the front-engined CVG6 and CVG5 were declining and the Daimler-engined CVD6 was in terminal tailspin.

By offering these models only with preselective gearboxes, Daimler was restricting itself largely to a diminishing proportion of the municipal market, and some big immediate postwar buyers like Newcastle and Edinburgh had already switched to Leyland. The launch of the semi-automatic Daimatic gearbox in 1957 helped stem the tide a little, but the introduction of the synchromesh-geared CSG models was probably too late to gain much new custom. Daimler needed to think big.

New management appreciated the challenge and, as the V8-engined SP250 sports car started changing the company's image in 1959, chief engineer Cyril Simpson – responsible for Daimler's cars and buses since 1919 – was persuaded to postpone his retirement to see through the revival of the bus range. The Fleetline, or RE30 as it was known briefly at its launch in 1960, is his lasting monument.

Simpson and his team took their cues from Leyland which had changed the rules of double-deck bus design with its rear-engined/front entrance 78-seat Atlantean prototype in 1956 and which had started building it in surprisingly large numbers from its launch in 1958.

Rather than just copy this new leader, they went one stage better, probably even two stages better. Production Atlanteans had a straight back axle, so the only way a 13ft 6in lowheight version could be built

*Coventry was an obvious customer for the locally-built Fleetline. Three Willowbrook-bodied examples sit at Daimler amid Fleetline and CVG6 chassis and Jaguar car shells.*

was by rather clumsily incorporating a nearside sunken gangway in the rear section of the top deck. The combination of the Daimatic gearbox and a drop centre back axle meant lowheight bodywork could go on the Fleetline without compromise.

**Prototypes**

The second stage better was the engine. Three prototypes were built with Daimler's obsolescent CD6 engine – only one (demonstrator 7000 HP) was bodied – but the big breakthrough when limited production began towards the end of 1961 was to use the Gardner 6LX instead, a highly-successful 10.45-litre version of the CVG6's 8.4-litre 6LW. The ingredients for success were in place.

Deluges of corporate good fortune also rained upon the new model. In May 1960, a few months before the Fleetline's launch, BSA sold Daimler to Jaguar for £3.4 million, taking its rival luxury car maker into the bus market for the first time. In October 1961, receivers were called in at Guy, Jaguar snapped up the assets and found itself with another range of buses and trucks to go with them. Among the easier tasks to be decided was the direction of double-deck design. Overlaps between the CVG6 and Guy Arab were largely eliminated and, faced with the choice of persevering with the Fleetline or trying to rescue Guy's clever, but decidedly troublesome front-engined/front entrance Wulfrunian, there was no contest.

Further luck came the Fleetline's way in June 1962 when Leyland took over AEC and dashed any chances there might have been for a rear-engined AEC double-decker. Daimler had a clear field to challenge Leyland for sales of high-capacity 'deckers and was helped by the operational superiority of a product that could take two heights of bodywork and appeared to be more economical to run.

**Long-lost**

By 1963, the Fleetline had caught up with the Atlantean and began outselling it in 1967. This product of a company with a hitherto dwindling following not only took Daimler into long-lost municipal fleets like Nottingham, Sheffield and Middlesbrough, but also won converts from other sectors that barely considered its offerings before. Right from the start, it secured big chunks of BET group business, some from companies that turned their backs on the Atlantean. By selling the Fleetline to Midland Red from 1963, it helped persuade that company to cease making its own double-deckers, depriving the world of the delights of production versions of the mid-engined D10.

From 1965, the Scottish Bus Group was added to the scalps on its boardroom wall, won over to the Fleetline after rejecting the Atlantean and experiencing serious problems with front-engined Albion Lowlanders it had persuaded Leyland to develop instead. That same year, London Transport bought eight Fleetlines and 50 Atlanteans, preferred the Fleetlines and – unable to get an equivalent AEC – bought another 2,646 between 1970 and 1978. The London Fleetline experience was lubricated by many tears, but by no means all were of Daimler's making.

Along the way, there were more clever adaptations of the Fleetline than Leyland ever dared visit upon the Atlantean. Walsall and the SHMD Board in Cheshire persuaded Daimler to develop a short version with its main door behind the front axle, there were examples with 6LW and Cummins V6 engines, longitudinal Cummins-powered 36-footers for Walsall and Johannesburg and various developments for single-deck bodywork. Some worked better than others, but none took anything away from the success of the core product, especially in the 1960s when it was still at the leading edge of bus design.

One of the finest compliments of all was paid to the Fleetline in 1964 when Leyland – realising the effect its unexpected rival was having on its own success – developed a lowheight Atlantean with the Lowlander's gearbox and, with great swallowing of pride, the Fleetline's gearbox.

**Audacious**

That combination won Leyland an audacious one-off order for a dozen from Daimler's home city of Coventry and helped hold Leyland's ground, but it was the best admission an arch-rival dared make that its competitor's product had at least one superior feature. And after Jaguar was merged into British Leyland in 1968 and Daimler and Leyland ceased to be rivals, it was the lowheight Atlantean that got the chop, replaced by the new option of a Leyland O.680-engined Fleetline.

Its defiance of corporate death saw the Fleetline through the 1970s when such tempests and vipers were thrown at it as the much-improved AN68 Atlantean, transfer of production from Coventry to Leyland, rebadging as a Leyland and an apparent fall in build quality. It continued to possess qualities customers found in neither Atlantean nor Bristol VR and its final snook cocked at Leyland was to provide the chassis development experience for MCW to call upon when it began developing the Metrobus in the mid-1970s and prevented the Titan from dominating the double-deck market.

The Atlantean may have broken the mould and shown the way in the late-1950s, but the Fleetline was the wonderbus of the 1960s which showed operators how good a rear-engined bus could be and which spurred its rival into further developing its products. Its success should be a source of pride to all who were involved in its development. **CB**

*The single-deck Fleetline was promoted as a means of fleet standardisation, and several operators took both single-deck and double-deck examples, like Huddersfield Joint Omnibus Committee (the legal lettering shows 'British Railways Board') whose 1968 SRG6LX example, No 29 with Roe bodywork, is seen.*

# Next Stop Please, Driver!

## Bristol memories from the years 1967-72, by NIGEL FURNESS

WHAT MAKES a man in his early forties with a young family and little spare time buy a 30-year old Bristol single-decker bus? Perhaps boredom, a desire for a new toy; or, having failed once at the preservation game, a need for redemption; or perhaps an attempt to keep alive the memory of a special time? Maybe there isn't a definitive answer, but I offer the following reminiscences in the hope that even if the answer does not lie therein, they may at least be entertaining and possibly informative!

### The beginnings

My earliest bus memory is of standing on the open platform of a double-decker in Bristol whilst my mother fought to fold up a pushchair. A later memory has me fighting with other boys for the privilege of using as a steering wheel the circular lower saloon heater in the ancient double-deckers employed by Chesterfield Corporation for school bus runs. Nevertheless it was the railway that captured my infant imagination; by the age of 10 I was a committed train spotter, spending hours beside the Bristol-Birmingham line. At 11 years old I progressed from local primary to grammar school in Bristol. Homework and long bus journeys left little time for train spotting, and more time was wasted chasing a mis-shapen ball around a field. A miserable time ensued, but something soon arrived to lighten the darkness! The seeds were sown on the 9 September 1967.

Boarding the lower saloon of an LD Lodekka in Bristol's Marlborough Street bus station after my first day at grammar school I encountered John, a classmate. Sharing a similar background and interests, we became firm friends. John had a strange hobby; when he saw a bus, he would write something in a notebook. When interrogated he explained that like locomotives, buses had numbers. Some numbers incorporated letters; an 'L' prefix meant they could go under low bridges, 'C' meant a city bus. Soon I was collecting the numbers too, but I wasn't really hooked until one afternoon in the bus station there appeared a huge, elegantly proportioned single-decker with a melodious transmission whine. 'Wow!' sez I, always a model of restraint, 'that's one of them Scandinavian 40-footers. Or is it 40-seaters? Anyhow, they're the latest thing'. My misguided enthusiasm for 'the latest thing' had confused this leviathan with the Leyland Panthers exported to Stockholm. John regarded me with a sympathetic smile. 'That, dumbo,' he said, 'is a Bristol RE-double-ell. We've got some RE-ell-aitches too; they're coaches.' 'Ah,' sez I, humbly. Impressed, I decided there was more to this bus spotting lark than met the eye, and determined to discover more. The 'we' John referred to was Bristol Omnibus Company, originally the Bristol Tramways & Carriage Company and affectionately known as 'the Tramways' by employees. Thus the company became the Tramways to us, and in the ensuing years we came to consider ourselves its most earnest champions.

*Preproduction Bristol Lodekka No L8133 in the yard behind Winterstoke Road (Bristol) garage after withdrawal. Note the later-type radiator grille (acquired shortly before withdrawal) and early type of destination display.*
J. Knox

Top: *Much excitement was caused when an anonymous 'diverted' Brighton, Hove & District VRT was discovered at the Central Repair Works.*
J. Knox

Above: *VRL/LH Prototype chassis No VRX002 HHW 933D slumbers outside the paintshop at the CRW after its spell of duty with Mansfield District. This bus was soon repainted in the stylish OMO livery and took fleet number C5001.*
J. Knox

## Loveable Lodekkas

The chassis of the handsome green buses that inhabited the city were built locally, by Bristol Commercial Vehicles (BCV) at Brislington. The bodywork was constructed at Eastern Coach Works (ECW) at Lowestoft, although there had been a Brislington Body Works (BBW). BCV had been part of the Tramways earlier empire, and this association made Bristol an interesting place in the late 1960s and early 1970s. The Lodekka prototype No LC5000 (LHY 949) had departed the streets some years prior to 1967, but the preproduction LD No L8133

(PHW 958) was still around, as was No 2800 (NHU 2), an LS prototype. John and I encountered both No 2800 and L8133 one rainy afternoon, forlorn and forgotten in the delicensed line behind Winterstoke Road garage. *Buses Illustrated* reported the withdrawal of No L8133 with the sombre words 'It has happened'.

Sombre words indeed; the possibility that I might not always be able to savour the characteristic creaking sound from the rear suspension of an LD was too awful to contemplate. The FLF Lodekkas did not inherit this characteristic but they had their own, like the sound of the transistorised inverters for the fluorescent lights, the high-pitched tone being immediately obvious as one set foot in the commodious lobby. 58-seat LDs with platform doors mingled with 70-seat FLFs on the 318 service from Bristol to the delightfully named town of Chipping Sodbury. This was our daily round trip, and the favourite seat in an FLF was over the rear wheelarch in the lower saloon, though goodness knows why as there was a good chance of being pitched into the gangway on fast corners!

### Rear-engined alluRE

From 1968 the Tramways bought large numbers of RELLs. The first batch (numbered in a new series from 1000) was decorated inside with green Rexine, white ceilings and blue Formica seat backs. Later deliveries had brighter furnishings, using cream Formica with a brown autumn leaf-like design. The driver's cab was also cream on these buses; this was soon painted matt black when drivers complained of night time glare. Saturday morning school (yes, really!) meant the 07.50 bus into Bristol. A regular RELL turn almost exclusively patronised by pupils from my school, we regarded it as our own private service. A friendly BCV engineer had taught us to distinguish the deep, muffled rumble of a Gardner from the high pitched rattle of a Leyland engine, so we would lurk behind the driver, encouraging him to wring every last ounce of performance out of the bus, whilst the tobacco (I think it was tobacco . . .) enthusiasts kept the engine company at the rear. Unfortunately I did not meticulously note the comparative performance of Gardner versus Leyland during these record-breaking runs, but I remember impressive performances from the RELL6Ls, 70mph being regularly achieved between Mays Hill and Coalpit Heath.

### Two doors in the City

A major event was the arrival of dual-entrance 44-seat REs for city routes 15 and 83. Country REs had worked these services since spring 1969. Some older REs were converted to dual entrance, and all subsequent city fleet REs were of this type. The front cover of the *Bristol Omnibus Magazine* for September 1969 depicted No C1114 (UHU 216H) and included a photo spread starring No C1118 (UHU 220H). The magazine described how the front door on these machines was controlled by a footswitch, the centre exit being controlled by a sixth position on the 'gear control switch'. These REs arrived wearing a livery of cream

MW5G No 2636 – the stimulus for the accompanying article – demonstrates the OMO livery applied to single-deckers from 1969, having lost its special City Centre Circle livery earlier in the year. Appropriately pictured outside the Bristol & West Building Society in 1970. The remnants of an advertisement for the B&W are still there on the boot lid today, the pencil lines used to guide the artist showing clearly through the remains of the paint!
Courtesy BVBG

No 2800 – the LSX prototype in the delicensed line at Winterstoke Road garage. Taken the same day as the picture of No L8133. The stylish curved windscreen line and complimentary winged motif were not, unfortunately, perpetuated on production LS types.
J. Knox

from below the windows to the rubbing strip with green roof and green skirts, a style applied to one-man operated (OMO) vehicles from early 1969. Most had Leyland engines; as deliveries progressed a modified body style with a curved windscreen and updated grille appeared. Opinions differ, but I preferred the squarer outline of the earlier flat-windscreen REs.

**Obscured by Clouds**

A feature of these new buses was sensational acceleration, aided by the power-assisted gear selector which allowed rapid upward gear changes, sometimes accompanied by violent jerks from the rear until the drivers became familiar with their new charges. The 15 route took me from school to Golden Hill, then a

beautiful green oasis in the city, now home to a superstore, for the despised ball-chasing. The 83 route took me to Eastville Park where I could catch a 318. A busy and congested route meant the acceleration of these vehicles was put to good use. The unsuspecting standing passenger could be unceremoniously catapulted 30ft down the gangway when an opportunistic driver stomped on the loud pedal! RE failures were rare but they did occasionally burst into flames. One morning we had to walk from Fishponds when the cab area of a Bristol-bound RE became obscured by clouds of smoke. Another RELL, No 1085 (OHW 597F), was later completely burnt out.

By this time the Leyland National prototype was on

Top: *Old stager GHT 127, back with the Tramways and carrying Badgerline fleetnames. After some years in the care of a preservation group, he (Prince Bladud!) carries fleetnumber 8583. Resting at Warminster on the occasion of the Warminster and West Wilts running day in September 1996, GHT 127 has now outlived most of those buses that were newly delivered in the year it entered preservation!*
N. Furness

Above: *L type No 2495 after entering preservation. During its first few years of preservation this bus carried the Bristol scroll fleetname, but is shown here carrying an earlier style of livery with painted fleet numbers as opposed to the later fleet number plates.*
J. Knox

the road, and soon RE production ended in favour of the National. Even so, the final RE count, including all variations, exceeded 400. Our Nationals arrived in 1973; we weren't impressed, but time has made me feel more charitable towards the old National. I can't forgive them for killing off the RE, but Leyland's fate was a punishment out of all proportion to the crime.

## Veterans

Leaving the 83 at Eastville Park we would wait for a 318 to appear beneath the Fishponds Road bridge that carried the former Midland Railway connection with the GWR Avonmouth line. The road under this bridge was lowered to allow the passage of trams, which was convenient for the replacement buses! The dip in the road remains, but the bridge has gone, as has the magnificent 13-arch viaduct just to the west, demolished to provide space for a superstore. Also gone are K5G LHU 982 (ex-No C3435), and KS5G LAE 316 (ex-No 3741), two veterans that would amble past whilst we waited. With LHY 929 (ex-No C3440) they provided staff transport for Brains of Mangotsfield, of Frozen Faggot fame.

A few L type saloons could still be seen; Elliots the road menders of Downend had two, LHT 911 (ex-No 2388) and LHW 908 (ex-No 2285), and there were two 'Queen Mary'-style coaches, NHY 942 (ex-No 2062) and NHY 947 (ex-No 2067) owned by Bensons the builders (Filton), and Robinsons of Mangotsfield respectively. By 1967 the Tramways had only three. One was 'preserved' No 2495 (LHY 976), a second was driver trainer W119 (LHY 974 ex-No 2493), and the third was tower wagon No W75 (FAE 60), its 1937 registration indicating a very early L5G.

The Tramways had considerable numbers of KSW double-deckers. These, like the K and L-types, had an unforgettable aural signature, a harmonious growl that increased in pitch as they accelerated away from a stop. I recently enjoyed the familiar melody again when I rode on GHT 127, the much-travelled 1941 K5G open-topper. GHT 127 appeared in the Central Repair Works body shop in 1969, after a sojourn with Brighton, Hove & District, and survives today in the care of Badgerline.

A number of lowbridge KSs, KSWs and LS saloons were converted to trainers during the period 1968-1972, giving these buses an extra few years' life and suggesting the Tramways were short of drivers, an impression reinforced by an advert with a 1930s style picture of a small boy wearing a busman's cap and swinging a conker (I could do that!) beside an RELL. The caption read 'My Dad's a Bus Driver'. What more could a boy want!

## Relics

Interesting relics abounded. Rogers of Chipping Sodbury had JO6A DHY 653 (ex-No 2201), long derelict after working as a mobile shop. Its BBW dual purpose body had a door set into its rear reminiscent of the corridor connection on a railway carriage. There was ex-Birmingham City Daimler COG5 EOG 183,

RELL, 1061 (NHU 195F), just arrived from ECW and another new RE with its BATH SERVICES fleetname displayed in slanting characters positioned (by mistake, I assumed!) over the wheelarch. This fleetname position became standard, and was applied to earlier vehicles with sometimes untidy results.

Entry to the CRW required charming our way past a gentleman in the Control Office. On special occasions (when we were extra charming), we were allowed to examine the vehicle ledger in the Control Office, where details of the Tramways fleet were recorded. Considerable kudos was accrued next day when we reported vehicle news back to other enthusiasts at school. Across the yard was the paintshop, where I recall watching advertisements being skilfully painted on the curved rear corner of a Lodekka. The buses were hand painted in their Tilling green and cream uniforms, and looked magnificent when newly treated. You could distinguish a new bus from a repainted one by the black beading that separated the green from the cream, a detail not perpetuated by the Tramways. The paint shop was both a source of wonders to behold and wonders to collect. The craftsmen often saved redundant items for us, so old fleet number plates, sections of destination blinds, even seat squabs were carted home to the amusement of regular passengers on the 318!

The body shop was the next stop, where carpenters and sheet metal workers wrought their magic on accident victims or rebuilds. We observed over several weeks the transformation of No LS 2844 (PHW 934) with white glazing rubbers, cream interior panels, fluorescent lighting and modern destination displays; when completed it was renumbered 3000. On one occasion we saw a boomerang-shaped MW that had been struck by a falling tree, on another the shocking remains of RELL fire victim No 1085. Its registration plate adorns my garage wall, a constant reminder of the dangers of fire.

### A Glimpse of the future

Disappointment experienced when our order for new VRT double-deckers was diverted to Brighton, Hove &

shorn of its upper deck, and a Bristol 4-ton lorry. There briefly appeared DDV 40, ex-Western National No 289, a prewar K reduced to a sad pile of scrap in a single day. At Frenchay another prewar K with BBW body was used as a building site office. This was identified as No L3909 by careful examination of the front dash panel. Its roof was used in the restoration of GHT 154 (ex-No C3336) by the Bristol Vintage Bus Group (BVBG).

South of the city the yard of Claverham Coaches contained L-type saloon JHT 827 (ex-No 2174) painted in pseudo-Tilling colours of bright green and cream, with all the interior woodwork newly varnished with gleaming polyurethane. The bodywork was jacked up at the rear on a pile of sleepers, causing it to take on a banana-like appearance!

### The Central Repair Works

Rainy Thursday afternoons would find us haunting the Central Repair Works (CRW) at Lawrence Hill. As well as vehicles from other operating districts there were often new deliveries. I remember a gleaming

22 (Lockleaze to Lawrence Weston) and 23 (Lockleaze to Shirehampton) services. To celebrate their arrival the Tramways issued a pamphlet instructing intending travellers in the correct use of the doors(!) and airing the company's motto (at least, I thought it was the company's motto) 'Please tender exact fare and state destination'. The pamphlets also contained engineering details of the buses and their cost – £11,000 each. They entered service on Sunday 23 July, 1972. The *Bristol Omnibus Magazine* for September 1972 noted this event, and the preservation of LS saloon No 2920.

**Homeward bound**

The homeward journey could be made using Stroud or Cirencester services. These followed a more rural route from Bristol, taking in the village of Westerleigh and the expanding housing estate at Yate. Dual-purpose MW6Gs with forced air ventilation and coach seats were the usual transport. These were popular because the high-backed coach seats provided a greater degree of privacy than usual, and this combined with the limited patronage of this service afforded the youthful Lothario the opportunity to woo the schoolgirl of the moment!

The MWs had narrow gangways, so I could hang forward from the two front seats and shout 'next stop please, driver' (an expression I had heard used by off-duty Tramways staff) instead of ringing the bell like any normal passenger. Beneath my feet the throbbing Gardner was gruff and friendly, whilst those MWs with exhaust brakes provided additional aural effects, particularly if the system was faulty!

From 1968 a City Centre Circle service had been operated by several MW5Gs painted in a special livery of cream with green skirts and window surrounds which greatly improved their appearance. The later standard one-man livery was derived from this scheme. The last two MW5Gs to join the Bristol fleet were Nos 2635/6 (HHW 451/2D). They were both deployed on the City Centre Circle and became familiar sights around the city centre, a sixpenny circuit from the Haymarket being a favourite trip when time allowed. The MWs became familiar and reassuring sights, especially when the Cirencester route was conveniently diverted past my home!

District in favour of RELLs turned to excitement when one was spotted at the CRW. Allegedly in for 'modifications', several more BH&D VRTs subsequently appeared. However, for excitement nothing compared with the winter's morning when, waiting for the bus to school, out of the mist loomed not the usual FLF but the unfamiliar visage of GGM 431D, one of two prototype VRLs.

The size, the unfamiliar pattern of moquette, the almost imperceptible engine noise from the wrong end and the strange shape of its destination box combined to strike an unforgettable note. It was an awesome bus, and a glimpse of the future. That journey passed too fast. This bus became No C5000, a fitting successor to the Lodekka prototype. Its partner, HHW 933D, became No C5001. Others obviously found them less impressive, as both had short lives with the Tramways.

Eventually the double-decker famine was ended; eight one-man-operated dual-door VRTs (Nos C5002-10 EHU 361K etc) arrived in the spring of 1972, painted in a special livery with a broad cream band between the decks, the lower deck copying the one-man single-deckers. The VRTs were employed on the

*25 years after being photographed outside the Bristol and West, No 2636 as she is today. Underneath the battered exterior there lies a strong heart, and she still carries many reminders of her earlier life including the special frames around the destination box added to carry the special City Centre Circle boards. Restoration of No 2636 to her 1968 condition is now well under way.*
N. Furness

## Lurking in the bus station

Any bus station is an interesting place for a bus enthusiast, and Marlborough Street was no exception. Express coaches from Red & White, Royal Blue, Bristol Greyhound and Black & White Motorways could all be found. I loved the Royal Blue livery, so imagine my surprise on finding a Lodekka in Royal Blue livery lurking in the bus station at Chesterfield! 10 DRB was Midland General no 461, so clearly the virtues of the Bristols were widely appreciated. No 461 later joined the exalted company of ex-Tramways Lodekkas in the West Riding Automobile fleet; an appropriate replacement for the revolutionary, if unsuccessful, Guy Wulfrunian.

The National Bus Company (NBC) enforced unimpressive livery changes. Cream was replaced by white which showed the dirt terribly. The famous Bristol scroll fleetnames were replaced by the corporate 'double-N' logo and fleetname style. Often only the fleetname panel was repainted in leaf green, giving a distinctly patchy appearance and the fleet started to look shabby. The worst atrocity was committed on the Bristol Greyhound coaches, where lustrous Tilling red gave way to ambivalent magenta. Initially a full-colour sprinting greyhound logo was employed, but the colourful canine soon changed to an albino one, then vanished altogether. This change coincided with the surprise arrival of two Leyland Leopards with Plaxton Panorama Elite bodies. We called them 'the Jukeboxes' because of their excessive brightwork.

## An ill-fated venture

I left school in 1974, other things took priority and in some ways it was the end of an era. One final act of

misguided enthusiasm remained to be played out; inspired by the writings of the late David Fereday-Glenn, I decided to become a preservationist. An attempt to purchase a Guy Wulfrunian in 1971 had elicited a polite letter from West Riding, thanking me for my concern and explaining that the Wulfrunians were still in use. This rebuff stiffened my resolve so John and I embarked on an ill-fated venture. In 1975 Elliots decided to sell its pair of 1949 L5Gs. Ted Amos (guiding light of the BVBG) bought LHT 911, which had a BBW body. The 2285 group was formed and bought LHW 908. A thorough survey was then undertaken, something we should have done earlier! The wooden-framed ECW body was rotten, and repair was beyond our limited abilities. There was some disagreement, and the 2285 group proceeded without the author and his comrade. No 2285's subsequent history was undistinguished. She languished for a time at Charfield station, home of 'The British Doubledecker', but I last saw her in a yard near Cromhall with her bodywork removed, and the end was obviously in sight. I was pleased to learn from Ted Amos that parts of No 2285 had been incorporated in the BVBG's latest project. Ted Amos passed away in July 1996, after a short illness. LHT 911 remains in the care of Ted's family. Ted also owned ex-Bristol Greyhound MW6G No 2138 (BHU 92C), which he bought out of service in the late 1970s. Restored by Ted to full Greyhound livery, No 2138 also survives with a new owner.

## The Lodekka's swansong, and another superstore

Gradually my beloved Lodekkas and REs disappeared from the streets of Bristol; lines of REs silently awaited their fate at the old Naval Stores Depot at

Wapley. The last FLF, No C7262 (GAE 883D), had something of a swansong. Repainted in Tilling green and cream, it spent its twilight years plodding up and down Muller Road on the 87/88 route where I would encounter it on my way to work. The 1980s saw the NBC livery replaced by playbus colour schemes and unfamiliar fleetnames. The old Bristols were replaced by smoky and uninteresting Mercedes minibuses. Bristol Commercial Vehicles donated its site for a desperately needed superstore and my interest hit rock bottom.

**Full Circle**

In summer 1995, I read in our local free paper that Badgerline was pensioning off its last REs, an event significant enough to be mentioned in the press. Suddenly it seemed my past was being pensioned off too. Persuading my wife I wasn't mad (difficult), and to lend me her expensive camera (easier), I pursued the last RE from Bristol to Wells. The driver probably thought I was mad too, as I repeatedly overtook him to find suitable locations for my pictures. Interest revived, an impulse purchase of *Buses Yearbook 1995* brought the activities of the British Bus Preservation Group to my attention; still inspired by David Fereday-Glenn's adventures in an open-top K5G, I applied for membership. The group's magazine arrived and there was HHW 452D (ex-No 2636) for sale in Nottinghamshire! A visit was arranged and on a foggy 2 December 1995 we (wifey and me) found an old friend slumbering in a Mansfield back yard.
Discovered in Scotland by Gavin Booth, not the editor, but another distinguished enthusiast with the same distinguished name, No 2636 had been a berry bus. We bought her on the spot, and I decided wifey must be mad too, as 2 December is our wedding anniversary!

Ian the vendor arranged delivery and we eagerly anticipated her arrival. All the memories returned as I travelled the last mile in No 2636. I couldn't resist the temptation to say 'next stop please, driver!' to the jovial Harry as we swept down my mother-in-law's drive. I became acquainted with Ted Amos in late 1995, and his advice and encouragement were invaluable during the first few months of owning No 2636. His was a great loss to the preservation movement. No 2636 is now but one metaphorical stop from home, for I intend her to return to Bristol when restoration is complete. We have both come full circle, which seems appropriate given No 2636's history, so this is as good a place as any to say 'next stop please, driver!'. **CB**

*I would like to express my thanks to John Knox of Dover for his assistance in the preparation of this article and for allowing me to include photographs from his collection.*

Nigel Furness has been a lifelong transport enthusiast, an interest which encompasses trains, buses, classic cars, and canals. Originally an electronics engineer, he now works in computing. From 1982 to 1995 he was a lecturer in a college of further education, then spent a year working as a software engineer at the University of Bath. He has recently returned to teaching and is head of computing and IT at Sandwell College in Bristol. He is married with two daughters.

The Bristol Omnibus Company empire probably reached its peak around 1968. Its operational area encompassed Bristol, Gloucester, Cheltenham, Bath, Trowbridge, Wells, Weston-Super-Mare and Bridgwater. The company's operations in Cheltenham were provided by the Cheltenham & District Traction Co, whose buses wore a smart dark red and cream livery and the fleetname 'Cheltenham & District'. In Bath, two companies were involved, the Bath Electric Tramways Co and the Bath Tramways Motor Co. Buses in Bath wore the standard Bristol livery of Tilling green and cream but carried the fleetname 'Bath Services'. In Gloucester the services were operated on behalf of the city corporation and bore standard livery but with the city's armorial device above the fleetname 'Gloucester'. In Bristol, the city services fleet was jointly owned by the city corporation, the distinguishing feature being the city's armorial device carried above the 'Bristol' scroll fleetname.

During the period covered by this article, the company reached a high level of standardisation on Bristol-ECW products with at one point all but one vehicle being of this manufacture. It then embarked on an ultimately disastrous policy of buying vast quantities of one-man operated single-deckers. Many had unnecessarily short lives, being replaced by one-man double-deckers during National Bus Company days.

*Timetable amendment No.4 announced the arrival of the eight VRTs for services 22/23 with a picture (presumably to aid identification of the new buses!), instructions for passengers, and a special technical note for bus spotters, who had obviously been noticed around the company's headquarters!*

**NEW BUSES ON YOUR SERVICE**

Amendment No. 4

On Sunday, July 23rd, 1972, your bus services 22 (Lockleaze to Lawrence Weston) and 23 (Lockleaze to Shirehampton) will be changed to one-man operation. This means that the buses will not have conductors and that your fares will be taken by the driver. Can you please help us by following the passenger code:—

• Please have your correct fare ready for the driver and state your destination.
• Please enter the bus by the forward door.
• Please leave the bus by the centre door.
• On single deck buses smokers please sit at the rear half.
• On double deck buses smokers please sit upstairs.

You will have brand new buses on your service. At certain times you will have the latest two-door double decks, and at others the new two-door single deck saloons — both types in the smart cream and green livery and offering a much higher degree of comfort.

**THE TIMETABLE**
There are slight changes to the timetable, and for your guidance we have printed the timetables in full in this free leaflet.

**TECHNICAL NOTES**
The new two-door double deck buses have a seating capacity of 70 (43 upper deck, 27 lower).
**Fleet Numbers** C.5002 to C.5009 inclusive. (Registrations EHU 361K to 368K inclusive).
**Engine** 6LXB Gardner, vertical rear transverse, developing 180 B.H.P.; 4-speed semi-automatic gearbox.
**Bodywork** Eastern Coachworks.
**Cost** £11,000 (subject to 50 per cent Government grant).

BRISTOL JOINT SERVICES.

mb d7435 6/72

The paintings of G. S. COOPER are a familiar and popular feature of Classic Bus magazine. For this book he has painted a scene depicting the Worcester Agreement. At Worcester the BET-owned tramways had been acquired by the Corporation, which had decided to enter into this agreement with the Birmingham & Midland Motor Omnibus company (BMMO, fleetname Midland Red) because it didn't want to operate its own buses. On 1 June 1928 Worcester City services were taken over and run by Midland Red, which drafted in its latest QL single-deckers. The Worcester Agreement was an historic one and formed the basis for many other agreements carried out by BMMO in its area.

# SOUTH WALES COMPANIES

R. L. WILSON photographs of company buses in South Wales in the 1950s and 1960s, when several territorial BET and Tilling group fleets worked beside some notable independents. Today, more than 30 years later, the ownership of the bus fleets in South Wales has changed dramatically

Above: *Red & White was formed in 1929 around existing companies and remained independent of the major groupings until 1950 when it sold out to the British Transport Commission, becoming a Tilling company. In 1978 it became part of the newly-formed National Welsh company, and the name survives as part of the Stagecoach empire. No S849, a 1949 Leyland Tiger PS1/1 with Lydney Coachworks 35-seat body, is seen in September 1956.*

Below: *Jones Omnibus Services of Aberbeeg dated back to 1921, and was purchased by National Bus Company (NBC) in 1969. Managed by Red & White under NBC control, it was merged into the ill-fated National Welsh company in 1978, and the name disappeared two years later. At the Jones depot at Aberbeeg in May 1970 is No 25, a very late-model (1969) Leyland Tiger Cub PSUC1/12T with 47-seat Willowbrook bodywork.*

Above: *Western Welsh started as South Wales Commercial Motors, and adopted the Western Welsh name in 1929 after the Great Western Railway bought a shareholding. It became a BET group company in 1931, and, under NBC control, was a major part of the new National Welsh company in 1978. Western Welsh was famous for its massive fleet of Weymann-bodied Leyland Tiger Cubs, and while at first glance this appears to be one of these, it is a Leyland Royal Tiger PSU1/13 with 44-seat Weymann body, one of 25 bought in 1951. No 424 is seen in St Davids in June 1954.*

Below: *The Rhondda Transport Company grew out of a 1908 tramway company, which briefly ran trolleybuses in 1914-15 and started operating motorbuses in 1920. A BET group company, it was under Western Welsh control from 1966, and the name has since reappeared. In the unusual dark green/cream coach livery in Porth depot in May 1970 is No 321, a Leyland Leopard PSU3/4R of 1968 with Willowbrook 49-seat dual-purpose body.*

Above: *One of Red & White's famous Duple-bodied Guy Arab IIIs, No L750, at Gloucester bus station in September 1959. New in 1950, the Duple lowbridge body had seats for 53.*

Below: *Looking odd in its independent-style livery in 1970, a year after passing into NBC control, No 27 in the Jones, Aberbeeg fleet, was a 1954 Bristol LS6G with ECW 45-seat bus body, new to the parent Red & White fleet.*

Above: *Western Welsh bought both AEC and Leyland double-deckers, including a batch of these shorter-length 68-seat AEC/Park Royal Bridgemasters in 1958/9. No 683, the first of the batch, is seen at Cardiff bus station in September 1959.*

Below: *In the 1950s Rhondda bought Leyland single-deckers and AEC double-deckers. No 422, a 1956 exposed-radiator Regent V with Weymann 61-seat Orion body, is seen at Cardiff bus station in September 1959.*

Above: *Thomas Bros (Port Talbot) was formed in 1951 by BET to bring together four independent operators in the Port Talbot area, and under NBC control Thomas Bros passed into an expanded South Wales Transport in 1971. In the 1950s its single-deck coaches were AECs and its single-deck buses Leylands. New in 1955, PTX 202 was a Tiger Cub PSUC1/1 with Weymann 44-seat body, and is seen in Port Talbot in September 1956. The Thomas livery was blue/cream.*

Below: *The South Wales Transport company was formed by BET in 1914, passing to NBC in 1969. Other local fleets absorbed into South Wales include James of Ammanford, United Welsh and Thomas Bros (Port Talbot). A staunch AEC customer, South Wales No 864 was a 1955 Reliance with 44-seat Park Royal body.*

Above: *James of Ammanford was a small company, BET-owned since 1950, which was absorbed into South Wales Transport in 1962, bringing unfamiliar Leyland types into the AEC-dominated SWT fleet. James No 218, a 1955 Weymann-bodied Leyland Tiger Cub PSUC1/1, is seen in September 1957 in Neath. The James livery was red/maroon.*

Below: *The Red & White group formed United Welsh in 1938 to bring together the activities of a number of its subsidiaries in the Swansea area. United Welsh was nationalised with Red & White in 1950 and, following the creation of NBC, it was acquired by the major local BET group operator, South Wales Transport, in 1971. This 1954 Bristol LS6B coach with 39-seat ECW body, is seen in September 1957.*

Neath & Cardiff Luxury Coaches Ltd had been BET-owned since 1952, operating express services between Swansea and Cardiff. TWN 558, seen in September 1962, was a 1959 AEC Reliance with Park Royal 41-seat body. Following the formation of NBC, the Neath & Cardiff business passed to South Wales Transport.

Thomas Bros 130 WNY, a 1964 AEC Reliance with Marshall 53-seat body, is recorded at Sandfields garage in October 1966.

United Welsh No 1243, a 1953 Bristol KSW6G with ECW 55-seat lowbridge body, seen in September 1959.

Above: *South Wales Transport No 607, a 1965 AEC Regent V with Willowbrook 64-seat forward entrance bodywork, seen in October 1966.*

Below: *West Wales Motors of Tycroes was formed out of a family quarrel in the late 1920s, and operated in the Ammanford, Llandeilo, Llanelli and Swansea areas. 600 ABX was a Leyland Leopard with 53-seat Willowbrook body.*

# MR LITTLE DISCOVERS THE TITAN

**Some municipal managers achieved fame and even notoriety. GAVIN BOOTH remembers a legendary Edinburgh manager and his legacy**

HIS NAME was on the side of all the trams and buses. 'W. M. Little, Transport Manager', it said. And his period of office coincided with the dawning of my interest in buses, so William Morison Little, usually known as Moris Little, became a boyhood hero, along with *Buses Illustrated* editor Alan Townsin, the Goons and William Brown of 'Just William' books fame.

And this is the door . . . Moris Little points to the glider doors on the first of 100 Weymann-bodied Leyland Tiger Cubs bought by Edinburgh in 1959-61.

Moris Little was already a personality by the time he reached Edinburgh. Although he had started his career in Edinburgh, fresh out of the local university, first with the Corporation's electricity department and then with the transport department, he had to move to gain promotion, and in 1941, at the age of 31, he became general manager and engineer of St Helens Corporation Transport – the youngest municipal general manager in the country. In 1945 he moved to Reading as general manager and engineer, but in 1948, following the sudden death of Robert McLeod, he returned to his home town as general manager of the transport department of the City and Royal Burgh of Edinburgh, to give it its Sunday name. And the Edinburgh job was a plum job; the Corporation was the seventh biggest municipal fleet in 1948, with 604 vehicles, 233 buses and 371 trams.

The bus fleet he inherited was largely made up of Gardner-engined buses. There were 159 Daimlers, mostly prewar standards, and during and immediately after the war Edinburgh had received 33 Guy Arab utility double-deckers, all with 6LW engines to tackle the city's hills, and there were 10 5LW-engined Arab IIIs delivered just before Moris Little took up his post.

Otherwise the buses were a mixed bunch, bought from necessity in the war and early postwar years. So there were utility Bedford OWBs, and Edinburgh's amazing collection of seven 'unfrozen' buses delivered in 1941/2, but few of these lasted very long in Moris Little's fleet.

### Splendidly non-standard

Edinburgh had staked a claim for anything it could get hold of in the bus-starved postwar period, so Moris Little inherited orders for 15 Bristol L6Bs and 17 AEC Regent IIIs, splendidly non-standard types which did nothing to get the fleet back to standardisation.

The first buses bought in Moris Little's time were four Crossley SD42/6s which had actually been ordered by Waldie of Helensburgh, but came into the Edinburgh fleet, re-registered, right at the end of 1948. In January 1949 orders were placed for 15 Guy Arab III double-deckers and 72 Daimler double-deckers. The first five Guys materialised in September, though the balance would not appear until January-May 1951. The Guys had Northern Counties bodies; Edinburgh had taken utility Arabs with Northern Counties bodywork, and the ruggedness of the combination doubtless appealed.

The 72 Daimlers ordered in 1949 were to dominate the bus fleet until tram-replacement Leylands started to pour in during 1954. The fact that they started to arrive just a month after they were officially authorised by Edinburgh Corporation tends to suggest that this was an order that had been in negotiation for some time. In a way they marked a return to the Daimler/Metro-Cammell combination favoured between 1935 and 1939, though not all had Gardner 6LW engines. The first 10 were CVD6 chassis, with

Passers-by gaze at the unusual sight of a rear-engined bus in Edinburgh, in February 1960. It was Leyland demonstrator 661 KTJ, a Leyland Atlantean PDR1/1 with Weymann semi-lowbridge bodywork, and was used on the 19 Circle, in common with most demonstrators at the time.
Gavin Booth

Daimler's own CD6 engine, but these buses were not as popular as the rest, which had Gardner 6LW engines, and were withdrawn a full two years before the contemporary Gardner-engined buses.

The Daimlers were almost to full Birmingham City Transport specification, apparently to speed deliveries, and although later in life – some lasted until 1967 – they would seem rather old-fashioned, they were well-regarded buses.

By 1951 the fleet had been significantly updated, with over 150 new buses delivered in a four-year

period, and Moris Little could turn his mind to another pressing matter – the replacement of the tramway system with motorbuses.

Edinburgh people liked their trams. So when in 1950 Little started to make noises about abandoning the trams in favour of buses, the locals were up in arms.

### Stately galleons

And why not? Edinburgh had a good tramway system. It covered much of the city, and the trams themselves were sedate, conservative four-wheelers – 'stately galleons' said one observer – that matched the mood of the place. New trams were still being built by ECT at Shrubhill, to a design that had first appeared on the streets in 1934, but the six built in 1950 were destined to be the last of the 84 domed-roof standards, and new investment in vehicles would be concentrated on diesel motorbuses. Although Little's 1950 report only recommended that the system should not be extended, and that 25% of the trams and of the system should be abandoned, it was clear that this was only the start.

The tramway system had reached its peak in 1937, and if World War 2 had not intervened, there would have been further extensions. The need for these extensions underlined Moris Little's problem. Edinburgh had been a relatively compact city when the basic tramway system had evolved in Victorian times, and its post-1920 expansion meant that sizeable new housing developments were taking place way beyond the tramlines. Right from the time they were built, buses served the big 1930s schemes, and the postwar growth of the city was planned for further-flung areas. Added to that was the need for extensive trackwork repairs, the fact that new trams were more costly than new buses (although trams lasted in service for 25-30

years, roundly twice the life expectancy of a motorbus), and the growth in private motoring, which meant that trams, running and loading in the centre of the road, were seen by some as a road safety hazard.

The first tram service to be withdrawn, in 1950, was hardly a contentious one, and the next withdrawal proposed by Moris Little concerned the route to Comely Bank, a branch line that affected no other routes. But a few weeks after the 24 tram had been replaced by the 29 bus, in June 1952, it was announced that the whole system was to close within three years.

### Hot potato

All hell was let loose, and the tram scrapping programme became a political hot potato. To no avail, because the replacement programme started in earnest late in 1952 and continued through to 1956 when the last two routes, 23 and 28, were converted to bus operation – although the Suez Crisis of that year did raise the possibility that the final closure might be postponed in the interests of fuel saving.

After 1952 the tram fleet quickly dwindled, to 285 in 1953, to 270 in 1954, to 170 in 1955, and to just 99 at the start of 1956, the final year. The growth in the bus fleet more than compensated for this: it rose from 349 in 1952 to 625 in 1956.

To replace the trams, and of course to allow for normal replacements of time-served buses, Edinburgh Corporation Transport bought no fewer than 485 new buses in the six years 1952-7. Although they were cheaper than new trams, this represented a substantial outlay but canny purchasing ensured that Edinburgh's citizens got value for their money.

Top: *The ultra-lightweight Orion PD2s confounded the critics by lasting for up to 21 years in everyday service. No 736, new in 1956, is seen at the Trinity bridge in July 1976, when cigarettes cost 33p and classified ads 93p. It was withdrawn later that year.* Gavin Booth

Above: *The traditional madder/white livery suited the Orion PD2s. No 572 is seen at Silverknowes terminus in 1975. New in 1955, it was withdrawn in 1976.* Gavin Booth

Moris Little was building a reputation as one of Britain's most progressive and adventurous transport managers. He favoured continental-style single-deckers with minimum seating and maximum standing space, a theme he would return to with his famous three-door Leyland Leopard, No 101. But in 1952 he bought 16 40-seat 'crush-loader' Leyland Royal Tiger single-deckers, Nos 803-18, and used some of these to replace the service 24 trams. They only lasted a matter of weeks on these duties, and were redeployed more sensibly, to be replaced by Leyland Titan PD2/12 double-deckers, from a batch of 21 bought that same year, Nos 240-60. Delivery of both the Royal Tigers and Titans started in January 1952, marking the start of a move towards a fleet that would be Leyland-dominated for the next four decades.

The Titans were an interesting purchase. Bought

from stock through Scottish Commercial of Glasgow, they are thought to have been a cancelled export order.

An 'odd' Leyland which passed through the ECT fleet at this time was No 185 (FOF 298), an ex-Birmingham Titan TD6C which had been fitted with an O.350 engine and Wilson preselector gearbox by Leyland as a test-bed for the model that would eventually appear as the Atlantean. ECT used the bus on loan from Leyland in 1953/4, and the bus returned to Leyland.

Although Moris Little clearly favoured Leylands, where previously the ECT fleet had been Daimler-dominated, the next 'new' buses were Guys. For £1,950 each, less than half the cost of an all-new bus, Edinburgh got 60 modern-looking buses in 1952/3 (Nos 301-60) that were to give up to 16 years' service. The Guy Arab chassis had been new up to 10 years previously with London Transport, part of LT's intake of wartime utility buses. ECT bought the chassis for just £250 each, scrapped the old bodies, refurbished the chassis, and had new 8ft wide Duple/Nudd 55-seat bodies fitted. Although these had rather basic interiors compared to previous Edinburgh buses, they were more than a ton lighter than the 1952 Leylands, and this was important in an era when fuel economy was important. No 314 is preserved at the Scottish Vintage Bus Museum in Fife.

The success of the Guys led ECT to carry out a rebodying exercise on 16 of its own wartime Daimlers (Nos 62-70/2-8). Again the old utility bodies were scrapped, new Gardner 5LW engines were fitted, and new 8ft wide bodies were fitted, this time by Alexander, ECT's first double-deck bodies from this Scottish builder. The Daimlers had a slightly shorter life than the Guys in this form; all had gone for scrap by 1967.

### Breathing space

The rebuilt Guys and Daimlers gave ECT breathing space, and allowed the first tram-bus conversions under the 1952 programme to take place. But new buses had been authorised in September 1953 at £3,659 10/- each, and these started to take the road in May 1954, in time for the withdrawal of the Corstorphine trams in July. These were Nos 401-500, 100 Leyland Titan PD2/20 with ultra-lightweight Metropolitan-Cammell Orion 60-seat bodies (Nos 480 and 487 were 63-seaters). Widely criticised at the time for their lack of heating and ventilation, and their spartan interiors (they weighed little more than 6.5 tons unladen), they went on to run for up to 22 years in Edinburgh – and many were then sold for further service throughout the UK.

Days after the first of the 100 Orions started to appear, ECT placed an order for a second batch of 100, and these started to arrive early in 1955, ensuring an almost constant supply of new buses for tram replacement. These buses, Nos 501-600, were subtly different: they had more ventilation than the first 100, and they had seats for 63 passengers.

Top: *Alexander-bodied Leyland PD2A/30 No 609 demonstrates the tilt-test mechanism in Shrubhill Works during an open day in November 1974.*
Gavin Booth

Above: *Late in its life Alexander-bodied PD2A/30 No 644 shows signs of patched paintwork as it climbs the North Bridge in March 1976, the year it was withdrawn.*
Gavin Booth

Newly-delivered Leyland Titan PD2/20 No 438 on a tram-replacement route in the summer of 1954. The lack of opening windows on its lightweight Metro-Cammell Orion body will be noted. A 1934 Metro-Cammell-built tram passes in the other direction.

One of the second batch of 100 Titans was delivered in unpainted Birmabrite finish, but No 575 had received a madder band when photographed turning into Princes Street. Ten more unpainted Titans were bought in 1957.
Ian Maclean

In April 1955 another 100 buses were ordered, but this time the order was split. There were to be 50 more Leylands, largely similar to Nos 501-600, and 50 Guy Arab IV with Alexander 63-seat bodies; no doubt ECT decided to dual-source to ensure deliveries in time to complete the conversion programme. Ten more Leylands were ordered in May 1955, and with the April order these materialised as Nos 701-60 between March 1956 and the end of the year. The Guys, Nos 901-50, arrived between November 1955 and May 1956.

The final tram-replacement orders were placed in November 1955, when the end of the tramway system was in sight. There were 40 more Leylands, which were delivered as 761-800 between November 1956 and November 1957, and 20 more Guys, Nos 951-70, which appeared between October and December 1956. The slow delivery of the last 40 Leylands, which arrived after the last tram-bus replacement, probably justified ECT's decision to buy the 20 extra Guys, which were delivered in a much shorter time.

So the last Edinburgh tram ran on the evening of Friday 16 November 1956, a sad night for the many thousands who recalled this reliable, high-quality system. The traditional British tramcar was definitely on its way out, and when Glasgow's last tram ran in September 1962, it only left Blackpool's famous seaside tramway, which of course survives to this day.

On the face of it, Edinburgh really didn't have much need for new double-deckers in 1957. It had the 370 tram-replacement Leylands and Guys, and so more than half of the 706-strong bus fleet was less than three years old.

But there were still older buses to replace, and the last 28 of the early postwar Guys bit the dust in 1957-62, along with some of the mixed bag of double-deckers ECT had scrambled to buy in those postwar years; so in a grand clearout the 15 Guy Arab IIIs, the 17 Daimler-engined Daimlers, and the 17 AEC Regent IIIs went for scrap – the AECs after only nine years in service.

But, truth to tell, ECT had over-stocked in the tram-

*The amazing No 998, the first of ECT's 81 forward-entrance Titan PD3s, and the only one to carry a Homalloy glassfibre front. It is seen in Queensferry Street on its usual route, the 19 circle.*
Gavin Booth

*No 999 should have had a Metro-Cammell body, but delays forced ECT to bring the chassis north to receive an Alexander body. When new it was painted all-red – with gold lining-out in true ECT style – and the squareness of the rear dome will be noted.*

replacement years, and had more new double-deckers than it really needed, so there wasn't the same urgency for new buses. And anyway, the ageing single-deck fleet was needing attention; the newest buses had been bought in 1952, and there was still a substantial fleet of prewar Daimlers ploughing round the 1 circle.

So ECT could easily have taken a break from buying double-deckers – except that the ground-rules were changing. The ink on the contract for the last batch of tram-replacement buses was hardly dry when the government announced that from July 1956 two-axle double-deckers could be 30ft long, 3ft longer than had previously been permitted. For Edinburgh and Moris Little, this was too good an opportunity to miss, and early in 1957 an order was placed for two Leyland Titan PD3s to the new length. These were to have forward entrance bodies by ECT's two main body suppliers, Alexander and Metro-Cammell, and the Alexander-bodied bus would appear at the Scottish Motor Show in Glasgow's Kelvin Hall in November that year.

### Much interest

There was much interest in the appearance of the new bus, which materialised as No 998. It was a Titan PD3/2, which meant that it had Leyland's pneumocyclic gearbox, fully-automatic in this case. The Alexander body was based on the design already familiar on ECT's Guy Arab IVs, but with the entrance behind the front axle. The front end was markedly different. Moris Little was an early proponent of glassfibre units on buses, which allowed easy repair and replacement. Leyland's own BMMO-style front was steel-built, so Little turned to truck cab-makers Holmes of Preston for a Homalloy front, a most distinctive structure that was to remain unique on No 998.

Inside, 998 had 72 seats (41 upstairs, 31 downstairs – later 42/30), and these seats were blue rather than the usual ECT maroon. The seat colour was chosen, apparently, because it had been intended to paint No 998 in the Edinburgh civic colours of black and white, already worn by the city's coach fleet. The bill for

and in 1958 Central SMT and Western SMT borrowed it. But ECT was keen to show No 998 off to its own passengers and in January 1958 it entered service on the 2, working its way through the double-deck routes, a week at a time.

The second chassis, No 999, sat at the Metro-Cammell factory at Elmdon, Birmingham, for some 18 months before ECT rescued it and passed it to Alexander at Stirling for bodying, along with four other Leyland PD3 chassis.

The five buses emerged in February/March 1959 as Nos 261-4, 999. Their bodies were similar to that on 998, but they had very square upper rear domes. They had standard BMMO fronts, though in glassfibre, and seated 72 (41/31). Nos 261-4 were PD3/3 models, with synchromesh gearboxes and vacuum brakes – in essence a longer version of the 300 PD2/20s; they cost £5,453 each, 15% less than 998. No 999 was another fully-automatic PD3/2, and was further distinguished by its livery – allover bright red with gold lining-out; it cost £5,934. Only one other bus was built by Alexander with this ultra-square rear end, a PD3 for Weardale Motor Services, registered 6 BUP.

The four ECT PD3/3s, numbered 261-4 to follow on from a batch of Leyland PD2/12s, were renumbered 994-7 in 1971 to release their original numbers for new Atlanteans.

**Livery experiments**

ECT was experimenting with liveries at the time, partly with a view to cutting painting time and introducing spray painting. One of the later Guy Arab IVs, No 959, appeared in an allover cherry red scheme in May 1959 (later relieved with white), and an older Leyland appeared briefly in all-madder with just a single white line later the same year. Shortly after, PD3 No 264 appeared in a variation of the standard madder/white application. Eleven of the Orion PD2s were delivered new in unpainted Birmabrite silver finish.

The livery experiments were inconclusive, and by 1962 all buses were in normal livery.

No buses at all had been bought in 1958, and 1959-61 darrivals were dominated by the delivery of the 100 Leyland Tiger Cubs with Weymann bodywork which were used to replace all of the older single-deckers.

The next new double-deckers were not, as had been expected, 30ft long PD3s, but marked a return to the 27ft PD2. The batch of 50 buses, Nos 601-50, were delivered from the end of 1961 through to March 1962. These had Alexander 66-seat (37/29) rear entrance bodies similar to the Guy Arab IVs, and were on PD2A/30 chassis, the equivalent of the vacuum-braked synchromesh box PD2/20s. These were well-finished and solid, and were popular buses.

They had been delivered with frames for the glassfibre St Helens-style front now offered on Leyland double-deck chassis, but had BMMO-style fronts fitted by ECT at Shrubhill before delivery to Alexander for bodying.

These were to be ECT's last traditional rear

Top: *Scottish Omnibuses borrowed 12 of Lothian's PD2A/30s in June 1977, initially to cover the annual vehicle shortage at the time of the Royal Highland Show, and surprised many by buying them in August. No 612 pulls out of Edinburgh's St Andrew Square bus station in June 1977.*
Gavin Booth

Above: *The spread of driver-only operation meant that the Alexander-bodied PD3s had relatively short lives. No 653, a 1964 PD3/3, is seen at Newhaven in July 1976. It was withdrawn the following year.*
Gavin Booth

No 998 was £6,470, exactly £2,000 more than the last of the MCW Orion-bodied Leyland PD2s which were being delivered just as No 998 was being prepared for the Kelvin Hall.

Other operators were keen to examine this new bus,

entrance buses, for the next order was for 30ft Leyland PD3s. Again 50 were ordered, and these were delivered in 1964 as Nos 651-700, costing £5,927 each. They had Alexander bodies seating 70 (41/29), and the rear domes were pleasantly rounded unlike those on their five predecessors. They were PD3/6s – essentially the same specification as the PD3/3s; the different designation was because Nos 651-700 were delivered with exposed radiators, and ECT fitted standard fronts before they went to the bodybuilder.

## Demonstrators

Moris Little was always looking at new types, and ECT had a stream of demonstrators over this period, none of which really influenced future orders. In 1957, 1958 and 1960, AEC Bridgemasters were tried; in 1957, two Daimler CVG6s, one a 30ft 6LX-engined bus; in 1959 a Walsall Dennis Loline; in 1960 a Leyland Atlantean; in 1960/1, two Guy Wulfrunians; in 1963, an Albion Lowlander. ECT had ordered a Lowlander chassis in 1961, when the model was announced, and the chassis arrived in Shrubhill early in 1962. It was still there two years later, and was returned to Albion in July 1964 to become Western SMT No 1085 (BCS 252C). Why so many of these buses were lowheight buses will shortly become evident.

But it was fast becoming evident that the PD2 and PD3 were becoming outdated, and the Leyland Atlantean, which Little's good friend Eric Fitzpayne

was buying in vast numbers for Glasgow Corporation, was looking like the bus of the future. ECT had tried an early demonstrator in 1960, but five years later decided to mount a proper series of tests to prove once and for all what bus was best suited to Edinburgh's conditions.

Three demonstrators were borrowed, an AEC Renown, Daimler Fleetline, and Leyland Atlantean, and these were matched against one of the 651 batch of PD3s. The Renown, with a front engine and forward entrance body, seemed to be the most outdated of the three demonstrators, for the Fleetline and Atlantean, rear-engined and with stylish bodies, by Alexander and Park Royal respectively, were crisp and fresh and modern. The tests used the buses on a series of routes, and passenger reaction was invited.

The PD3 and Renown, perhaps inevitably, came out worst. There was very little between the Atlantean and Fleetline, and ECT recommended that 25 of each should be bought, but conservatism ruled and the next order for 50 buses was split equally between Atlanteans and PD3s.

The PD3s came first, and were used in August 1966 to double-deck the 1 circle route, which from its introduction as service 1 in 1919 had been single-deck because of low bridges at various points on its route. Now bridges had been removed or roadways lowered, and this busy route could now be operated by double-deckers, and the new PD3A/2s, Nos 826-50, were most

Top: *Newly-delivered PD3/3s outside Shrubhill Works in the summer of 1964, with a similar chassis on the right ready to go to the Alexander coachworks at Falkirk for bodying.*
Gavin Booth

Above: *The final batch of PD3s, delivered in 1966, differed only slightly from the 1964 batch. No 840 in Princes Street when new, passing a site now occupied by British Home Stores.*
Gavin Booth

regularly associated with this route.

Unlike Nos 651-700, which they resembled, the new PD3s had been delivered with frames for the St Helens-style glassfibre fronts now offered by Leyland, and ECT fitted Midland Red-style fronts before they went to Alexander's coachworks for E type bodies.

**New era**

The first ECT Atlantean, No 801 (now preserved) had been shown at the 1965 Scottish Motor Show, and the production batch, Nos 802-25, followed hard on the heels of the PD3s. A new era had dawned in Edinburgh, and the Atlanteans would dominate the

fleet through the 1970s and early 1980s until the Olympian took over. As this is written there are just a handful of the more recent Atlanteans left in service, and the next delivery of double-deckers will doubtless see them off.

Withdrawal of the 'in-betweenies' – the buses bought between the tram-replacement buses and the first Atlanteans – started in 1974, when 998, still with its unique front but with standard red seats, and the other five earlier PD3s, Nos 994-7 (originally Nos 261-4) and No 999, were withdrawn and, somewhat surprisingly, sold for further service to Highland Omnibuses where they ran for a couple of years before sale to an Essex dealer. Most saw further service, and 998 was saved for preservation for a while, but appears to have been scrapped.

The rest of the 'in-betweenies' survived into Lothian Region Transport control in 1975, but not for long. The PD2/30s, Nos 601-50, quite late examples of a type that was fast becoming obsolete outside London, were withdrawn and sold in 1976/7, 12 of them, amazingly, bought by Eastern Scottish for further service. The 75 PD3s were withdrawn between 1975 and 1980, as the conversion to driver-only operation was completed, and No 665, now preserved, was Edinburgh's last crew-operated bus.

The PD3s were an uneasy bridge between the high-capacity 27ft long buses, seating 63 or 66 seats, and the 75-seat Atlanteans, which looked modern and allowed driver-only operation. With just 70 seats, a longer bus, and awkward entrance arrangements, the PD3s were possibly not the best buses Edinburgh has ever bought, but in a way they were overtaken by events, which meant that the lives of some – the 1966 deliveries in particular – were short by Edinburgh standards, barely 12-13 years.

Moris Little's Leyland legacy lasted long after he had left ECT to become chairman of the Scottish Bus Group. ECT and its successor, Lothian Region Transport, resisted the attractions of the various double-deck models that were on offer in the 1970s and 1980s. It tried Ailsa, Metrobus and Scania N113 demonstrators, and even ordered two of Leyland's TN15 Titans – but that order was cancelled. It moved seamlessly from Atlanteans to TL11-engined Olympians, to Cummins-engined Olympians, to Volvo-engined Olympians.

Things would surely have been different if Moris Little's career had taken a different direction in 1948 . . . **CB**

*Gavin Booth, editor of the bi-monthly* Classic Bus *magazine, is a well-known writer with many bus books and articles to his credit. Married, with two grown-up children, he is also involved in church work, and writes musicals.*

# GREATER MANCHESTER'S LAST CLASSICS

## SELNEC PTE inherited an amazing variety of buses from the municipal fleets that formed it. Some of these, DAVID THROWER reckons, were classics

*Ex-Manchester 1958 Leyland Titan PD2/40 No 3478, still in red, emerges from the Fairfield Street tunnel beneath Manchester Piccadilly station – complete with the customary throaty exhaust effects – on the joint Ashton/Manchester /Salford route from Ashton bus station to Peel Green.*
David Thrower

IF THE 1950s marked the high noon of the all-time great classic designs of bus, then for most of us the 1970s marked their sunset, with the age of the halfcab and the open back platform ending for ever – the immortal Routemaster excepted. For many, the disappearance outside London of familiar conductor-operated designs was to bus travel what the disappearance of steam had been to rail enthusiasts. Not quite as cataclysmic perhaps, but the nearest equivalent with the future, however efficient, made up of . . . well, each to their own opinion . . .

However, even the 1970s still held quite some degree of aesthetic interest in one or two areas,

perhaps nowhere more so in the UK than in Greater Manchester. True, London had a great quantity with its swarms of Routemasters and stubborn if increasingly scattered pockets of resistance of RTs and RFs, the RTs in particular making a brief but very welcome comeback in the West End in mid-decade.

But Greater Manchester still had both quantity and variety, something that had disappeared by the early 1970s or even earlier, at least insofar as classics were concerned, not only from the large tracts of what had become NBC territory but also from some quite major towns and cities, where more traditional designs might have been expected to have lasted longer.

The GM phenomenon was in part due to the very mixed and highly individualistic inheritance of the Greater Manchester Passenger Transport Executive and its immediate predecessor, Selnec. These had been bequeathed by a multiplicity of predecessors – the Manchester City and the Salford City Transport fleets, Bury, Rochdale, Oldham, Ashton, Stockport, Wigan, Leigh and Bolton Corporations, Ramsbottom UDC, the SHMD Joint Board, North Western Road Car, Lancashire United and the odd independent. These fleets, totalling around 3,000 buses, were still providing quite a meal for the engineers and administrators to digest, and it was to be some years before standard livery and even longer before standard designs of bus completely took over.

### Prosaic and plebeian

The more committed local enthusiast in Manchester was apparently still lamenting the Crossleys and Daimler COG5s (as a non-native moving into the region, I have to confess that I had no clear idea what a *Cog-Five* was exactly, but tried to look suitably reverential) to make a deal of fuss about anything so prosaic and plebeian as the surviving Leyland PD2s and PD3s. The Crossleys in particular seemed to have an especially devout following, despite having long since been recycled into kitchen implements and other more useful mundanities (all that engine oil consumption!), and their sacred memory still hung over the city like some ghostly and unseen presence. One almost expected a few to re-appear on football extras during winter fogs, only to disappear again with spectral crews afterwards . . .

The trolleybus, meanwhile, and enthusiast fixation with it, had perhaps never really caught on in the area, though a few poles survived in silent reproach in Piccadilly Gardens and elsewhere as lamp standards. Paradoxically, Manchester's trams (the first lot)

Top: *Rare ex-Manchester Leyland Titan PD2/34 No 3520, with characteristic Burlingham bodywork, dumped in the scrap line behind Hyde Road works, awaiting its fate in 1976.*
Warren Vipond

Centre: *Its fate happily turned out to be preservation, and in 1986 it was photographed, back in Manchester colours, at Laxey, on the Isle of Man.*
David Thrower

Left: *While most of the ex-Manchester Burlingham-bodied Leyland Titan PD2s were synchromesh-box PD2/40s, six were PD2/34s with pneumocyclic transmission, including No 3517, seen in Piccadilly in GM livery.*
David Edwards

seemed to enjoy greater residual respect. Truly startling later events, such as the arrival of bouts of Routemasters and Italian-built light rail vehicles, remained undreamed of, although a lone RM had once appeared for trials in the early 1960s.

This, then, was the backdrop to the decline and fall of classic buses from one of the most interesting areas in Britain for bus operations.

The Greater Manchester area had played a significant part in the general nationwide move to eliminate the traditional double-decker, having included among its local constituents some of the last purchasers of such designs. Two personalities in the transport world had particularly significant roles in terms of bringing forward replacement designs. Ralph

Bennett's tenure at Bolton and later at Manchester City Transport was highly influential in the drive for the high-capacity 'new look' one-man double-deckers, incorporating pay-as-you-enter.

The initial designs for Bolton tended towards the boxy, if in a very attractive burgundy/cream and, in some cases at least, with sloping window pillars. But when Bennett moved to Manchester, an especially inspired and striking design was produced by Ken Mortimer and approved by Bennett after some initial resistance from the more conservative elements of the manufacturing industry. This was to become the well-known 'Mancunian', and its tasteful initial red/white livery and extremely large and deep wrap-round windscreen was to create an almost futuristic image

Above: **Newly painted in GM livery, ex-Stockport Leyland Titan 1962 PD2A/30 with East Lancs 60-seat body, No 5957, in Manchester's Stevenson Square. The St Helens-style glassfibre front was fairly rare in the Manchester conurbation; most operators preferred to stick to Leyland's exposed radiator.**
David Edwards

Left: **Ex-Ashton Corporation No 5447, a 1965 Leyland Titan PD2/37 with 65-seat Roe forward entrance body, at Manchester Victoria station, on the trunk 218 service from Manchester.**
David Edwards

that looked modern right up until final withdrawal in orange/brown in the 1980s. The appearance of such buses in the more progressive fleets in significant numbers gave chrome-radiator PD2s a decidedly 'jalopy' image, to be expunged as soon as possible in the search for progress.

## Salcunians

The first Mancunians had arrived in February 1968. Manchester City Transport was to disappear as an organisation by October 1969, but not before Salford

City Transport next door had also placed an order for 20 buses (locally termed 'Salcunians' by enthusiasts) and perhaps more might have followed. However, the newly-formed Selnec Passenger Transport Executive decided to draw up a specification for a new standard bus, based upon existing Park Royal/Roe/Leyland/ Daimler combinations, and, after a brief period of experimentation, large numbers of 'Standards' appeared. Over the next 10 years, these were to eliminate almost everything of traditional enthusiast interest from the Greater Manchester scene, perhaps rather in the way that the RT and RTL had done in London in the late 1940s and early 1950s for an earlier generation.

Not that the successive onslaughts of the Mancunian and the Standard were to be pitched against a particularly vast remaining army of 'crocks'. A number of the municipalities in the region had implemented programmes of purchasing rear-engined buses well back into the 1960s. Apart from already-mentioned Bolton, Bury had bought a batch of Atlanteans of Liverpudlian-style appearance (one of which is preserved), and Rochdale had a number of Fleetlines, as had SHMD.

Oldham and Ashton had batches of Atlanteans to locally-specified bodywork styles. Manchester and Salford also had batches of Atlanteans and Fleetlines, some to the 1950s slab-fronted styling, and again examples have been preserved. North Western was to bring some lowheight Fleetlines and Bristol VRTs, never a common type in this area. And the later addition of Lancashire United brought in further batches of Fleetline, although in the case of LUT these were more than swamped by an armada of 146 Guy Arabs, almost half the total LUT fleet, that accompanied them. Wigan's Leylands still looked superb, an asset to any fleet, but were slowly on the way out.

A handful of operators stood out against these rear-engined converts. Leigh Corporation, albeit a small fleet, had no rear-engined deckers, nor had even smaller Ramsbottom, whilst Stockport was the most prolific PD user of all, its own batch of Bristol VRTs having been incinerated at a works fire at East Lancs before delivery. In fact, Stockport had so many PD2s and PD3s that rumour had it that they were still secretly assembling them themselves somewhere, from stored CKD kits – a sort of 'Ashok Mersey Square' . . .

## Most prolific

The PD2s and PD3s were by far the most prolific of the traditional survivors in Greater Manchester. As late as 1975 the Titan could still be found in most parts of the county, particularly Manchester, Salford, Wigan and the aforementioned Stockport, but with smaller contingents in almost all the surrounding towns. For those few dwindling years, the throaty and harsh roar of the O.600 engine and the image of halfcabs, sweeping wings and front-end radiators could still be

savoured. And some of these types fitted so well into their surroundings, such as the locally-bodied Northern Counties and Massey PDs in Wigan, with engines and chassis from only a few miles further north. Local buses created jobs for local people! Such buses were part of a way of life and exuded civic pride. Not for nothing had the buses of Wigan, to take that example, once featured miniature green lights to either side of their destination screens to tell passengers that this was one of their buses.

Such civic allegiances lingered later than one might think. The writer remembers older passengers on a Salford overspill estate in 1976 boarding a cast-off Atlantean from the Manchester fleet (how they kept breaking down!) and complaining that it had cloth seats. They didn't want cloth seats! Green leatherette was good enough for them, and always had been. Give them back a Salford PD2 (and preferably not in that new-fangled orange) and they would have been happy. And, no doubt, Woodbines would have reverted to fourpence a packet.

The other minority chassis types gave some much-welcomed variety to the Titan diet. Apart from the redoubtable Guy Arabs to the west, there were pockets of AEC Renowns in Leigh and down to the south in North Western territory, the much-admired AECs at Rochdale, a small number of Dennis Lolines (by now limited to North Western), and modest numbers of Daimler CVG6s and a handful of CCG6s. As late as 1976 Salford's fleet included a pair of front entrance crash-box CCG6s, which were regarded at the garage as the 'booby prize' and were a real embarrassment to unwary drivers becoming all too used to semi-automatics. Experience recalls one of the crash-boxes in its last weeks being driven on an entire round trip to Bury in third gear only, its driver hopelessly unable to effect *any* changes, let alone noiseless ones. Even the hill-starts were in third, the resultant thick brown smoke from the clutch coming up through the floor into the lower saloon to the alarm and amazement of the passengers, as the bus juddered slowly into motion.

## Tasteless

Although many of the surviving makes of bodywork were by this time only to the basic (sometimes very basic) MCW Orion style, even this had some limited appeal (remember, by then this was the tasteless seventies, of Bay City Roller and platform shoe; all appeal is relative) and there was much else besides to interest the discerning eye. The products of Northern Counties, Burlingham, Massey, Longwell Green, East Lancs, Weymann, Roe, Alexander . . . still quite a respectable list for the twilight years of the Great British Bus Industry. And quite old-fashioned styles could still be found in some places. The Stockport East Lancs contingent in particular exhibited bodywork that hailed from another age, whilst some might have maintained that the gaunt bodywork of one of Stockport's surviving Longwell Green products hailed from another planet. Other individualistic features still around included Salford's cumbersome externally-mounted destination gear, always an open invitation to unauthorised twiddling, and Manchester's home-made Daimler radiator cowls on its MCW and Burlingham survivors, perhaps faintly reminiscent of a prewar radio speaker. These looked particularly odd on the

Above: *Wigan's buses always looked immaculate in their rapidly-disappearing maroon/white livery, worn here by No 3218, a 1960 Leyland Titan PD3/2 with locally-built Northern Counties 70-seat forward entrance body. Only the fleetnumber vinyl indicates that it is in the GM fleet.*
David Edwards

Above Left: *The former Salford Daimlers were numbered from 4001, seen here displaying the unusual Salford destination gear to good effect. It was a 1962 CVG6 with MCW 65-seat forward entrance bodywork. The FK garage code signified Frederick Road, Salford.*
David Edwards

Left: *The redoubtable Guy Arabs of Lancashire United Transport were a popular sight for many years. No 281, a 1967 Arab V with Northern Counties 73-seat body, one of the last Arabs to be delivered to LUT, is seen at Greengate, Salford.*
David Edwards

Burlinghams, the rounded-top grille clashing with the very square upper-deck front elevation. It is a pity indeed that one was not preserved.

There were also a few other odds and ends around, outside the main GMT fleet, mainly in non-passenger use. Manchester City Council's recreation services department ran a small fleet of MCW and Burlingham Leylands as mobile toolsheds, some fitted with power-operated side ramps for loading lawnmowers. Salford's Frederick Road garage boasted an ex-Liverpool tin-front PD2 as a playbus and, high in the Pennines to the east, a Southdown 'Queen Mary' in its glorious original colours could sometimes be espied in the Diggle area on school contract work. The absorption of a small independent, Godfrey Abbott Group, into the PTE

Top: *Against a mill background typical of its home territory, ex-Rochdale No 6209, a 1957 AEC Regent V/Weymann, represents a chassis type that was rare in the Manchester area.*
David Edwards

Above: *Leigh Corporation and North Western contributed AEC Renowns to the Selnec/GM fleets. At Leigh bus station is ex-Leigh No 6915, a 1965 Renown with East Lancs 72-seat forward entrance body.*
David Edwards

fleet briefly bought an Albion Lowlander into the fold, though regrettably it saw no further passenger service. And, of course, there were the dwindling remnants of the AEC Regents of A. Mayne & Sons, with their Oxfordian livery, to add further interest.

Inevitably there has been a tendency in this monograph to focus on double-deckers, single-deck halfcabs having long since departed Greater Manchester (though not nearby Burnley, Colne & Nelson) by the 1970s. However, some brief reference is justified to some fairly-traditional-looking Tiger Cubs on the Stockport and North Western fleets and some Rochdale Reliances that survived until the middle of the decade, along with a small batch of similar buses in Wigan. They at least sounded classical! Few if any of other single deckers had any traditional appeal, at least to this writer, and of course saloons were in any case very much in a minority in this agglomeration of urban landscapes.

We all had our favourites. Ashton's Titans had strikingly-attractive blue interiors with swirly-patterned seats, Manchester's had gurgling exhausts, especially for some unknown reason the Burlingham batch, and retained a peculiarly archaic air, with grime-blackened upholstery, whilst Wigan's always looked immaculate in their rapidly-disappearing maroon/white livery. Lancashire United was . . . well, Lancashire United, and wasn't that something special enough in itself? 'Just the Job - a Job at LUT', as the recruitment posters said.

### Solace

But standardisation marched remorselessly onwards. A source of some solace to the observer of the time was the way decline in one area would be offset by the transfer of some of the classic remnants to another patch for a few months' further service on peak extra and 'floater' (rush-hour standby) duties. This was to develop into something of a moving battle, with Salford's Leylands migrating uphill to Oldham, Stockport's moving eastwards to Ashton-under-Lyne, Wigan's, Ramsbottom's and Leigh's coming up-town to Manchester, and some of Manchester's covering for shortages in, need one say it, Salford . . .

Such machinations produced some real if short-lived treats for the enthusiast, with Wigan-liveried Titans looking more than lost in South Manchester's suburbs, Manchester's red appearing in unexpected parts of rival Salford and, most remarkably, a Leigh Corporation lowbridge PD2, complete with sunken gangway and quadruple seats, working on a rush-hour journey from Manchester to Bury. This for the uninitiated would be akin to Addlestone's last green RLH putting in a guest appearance down Whitehall on the number eleven . . .

Several species stood more-or-less aloof from these protracted manoeuvres. North Western's Lolines quietly expired almost unnoticed in their home territory, as did Rochdale's splendid Regents, and likewise the attractive Renowns at Leigh faded out on

home ground, though by now such 'lasts' were beginning to be noted and commemorated in a modest way by those in the know. Above all, the ubiquitous Lancashire United Guy Arabs – ubiquitous, that is, to LUT's state-within-a-state operation – to my knowledge never strayed outside their home territory, which was admittedly far-flung enough to embrace Warrington and Liverpool. Personal experience does, however, recall one isolated exception to this rule, on a hot summer evening in 1976 that had proved a trifle too hot for a Salford one-person operated Atlantean which had packed it in at Manchester Victoria. Its incredulous driver was given a smart red Guy Arab front-loader plus LUT conductor as replacement,

which to his credit he accepted as the joke it was, even if his knee-muscles reputedly required a medical afterwards and the passengers *en route* to Bury shunned it in disbelief.

**Rapid extermination**

By this time the process of extermination of interesting types had become very rapid, accentuated in its morbid fascination by the thought that this really was going to be the end of an era that could be traced directly back to the Leyland TD1, and its Dennis, Crossley, Guy and Daimler equivalents. And in the northwest this was being made all the more interesting due to the loss of links with former operators.

*Everything stops for tea. This ex-Leigh Corporation 1958 Leyland Titan PD2/30 with East Lancs body ended its career as a driver trainer and is parked outside Manchester's Hyde Road garage for a brew.*
David Thrower

The fate of the older halfcabs was sealed with the vast batches of Selnec/GM standards bought from 1972. The first prototype, originally No EX1, was shown at the 1970 Commercial Motor Show. It was a Leyland Atlantean PDR1A/1 with Northern Counties body.
Gavin Booth

1974 had seen the end of North Western's and Leigh's Lolines and SHMD's Titans. The following year was to see off Bolton's last CVG6 and the final link with Crossley Motors, the Crossley-bodied survivors in the Stockport fleet. But if one year marked a turning point it was to be 1976, of record-temperature fame. With standard types arriving in full spate, combined with service cuts and other savings, the halfcabs took a real pounding. Despite the compensations of a limited programme of recertifications of Stockport, Manchester and Salford PD2s and the arrival into the main fleet of the Arabs, there was a sharp and very visible reduction in interest for the traditional enthusiast, including the final removal of the Burlingham PD2s from the Manchester fleet and the Roe PD2s from the Ashton fleet. This period marked the start of a flurry of preservation bids, as it was going to be 'now or never' in most cases.

The years 1976-7 saw this onslaught focused increasingly on the Leylands, but included Salford's last Daimler back-loader, happily to be rescued by transport historian Ted Gray and restored to its original splendour. But type by type they disappeared, until by the end of the decade it was all over. For once, more than just photographs and memories have survived, however, and due to the foresight of the Passenger Transport Executive's then marketing manager, Roger Bowker, an excellent representative cross-section of buses was set aside and restored at each 'home' garage to form the nucleus of what is now the Museum of Transport. **CB**

*David Thrower worked as a transport planner for a number of local authorities and passenger transport authorities, and has been actively involved in the preservation movement.*

# DOING THE RIGHT THING

## MICHAEL DRYHURST investigates a US transit agency and its UK connection

**W**ALK INTO the Davis, California domain of Unitrans general manager James McElroy and you could be forgiven for thinking you'd been 'Dr.Who-d', inasmuch as the walls of the office complex – despite the fact that Mr. McElroy is American and has served much time in other transit agencies in the western United States – are covered in Anglophilia, 'Come to Britain' posters, 'Kew Gardens by Tube', pictures of prominent UK buildings and landmarks plus posters of Unitrans itself, all of which latter feature a stylised rendering of a bus . . . a British bus, an RT . . .

Unitrans has maintained a British connection ever since its inception over 30 years ago in 1967. If you

Above: **The two buses that inaugurated the ASCUD Unitrans services were ex-London Leylands Nos RTL1014/1194, purchased in 1967. No RTL1014, seen here, still serves Davis. Its existing O.600 engine may be replace by a Cummins.**

All photos by Michael Dryhurst

Right: **With diligent maintenance and thoughtful scheduling, Unitrans has managed to extract a much greater life out of many of its vehicles. One such is No 4508, a GM TDH4512 which first entered service with Sacramento Regional Transit in 1958 and was sold to Unitrans on withdrawal in the mid-1970s. Withdrawn in 1997, its sister No 4507 was donated to the Pacific Bus Museum; No 4508 soldiers on.**

*Listing heavily to starboard as it turns into Russell Boulevard carrying rush hour passengers is No RT742, one of two Saunders-bodied RTs in the Unitrans fleets, and the only one to retain its roofbox indicator.*

thought all of those Sandra Dee, James Dean, Troy Donohue, or even many Elvis Presley movies of the mid-1950s and 1960s were amiss in their portrayal of American teen-life, particularly with regard to 16-year old youths owning cars, you could be wrong; the great social make-up of the United States is the mass middle-class (needless to say, in the United States national demographics are determined by financial standing, not birthright!), and virtually all US middle-class teenagers, while still studying, inevitably take a part-time job to enable the purchase of (a) parental independence and thus (b) a car. So it is the norm for American kids in their mid-teens to own a car, and has been so since the end of World War 2.

The Association of Students at the University of California, Davis (ASUCD), is the parent body of Unitrans, which latter came into being as 'University Transport Systems'. ASUCD is a sort of student-elected watch committee which safeguards many aspects of life on the Davis campus. By 1967, the principals of ASUCD were worried at the number of students' on-campus cars and although the state had initiated its anti-smog programme in 1966, only cars built in the 1965 model year and thereafter were fitted

with anti-smog devices. Pollution from student's cars was becoming a major problem as was that of insufficient campus parking lots to accommodate the influx – added to which there was the congestion experienced in Davis itself, compounded by the student vehicle-parking at their accommodation, which was spread all over the city. So. ASUCD resolved not only to tackle the problem, but to contain it and . . . reduce it.

But how?

**Best course**

It was decided that the best course was to provide a bus service between the various halls of residence and the campus itself, but even the youthful officers of ASUCD were astute enough to realise that not just any old bus was going to attract students out of their cars and whatever was provided, it had to be different. And so, in the early summer of 1967 ASUCD contacted UK dealer PVS of Canvey, Essex, and purchased two ex-London Transport Leyland Titan PD2/1 7RT double-deckers, to inaugurate the Campus bus service. Nos RTL1014 and 1194 eventually arrived in Davis in late 1967, and in February 1968 the service was launched. Apart from conforming to California law concerning marker lights on the extremities of commercial vehicle bodywork the two Leylands were not modified in any way for their new, transatlantic role. The right-hand driving position remained unchanged as did, more importantly, the left-hand loading area. However, as passengers would be

Top:: *Although withdrawn by Unitrans as long ago as 1981, the former London Nos RLH21 and RT3752 have reappeared within the last couple of years at Sheldon, in south Sacramento county, minus their engines.*

Above: *Looking resplendent after a body rebuild and repaint is RT 4573, the only Weymann-bodied bus in the Unitrans fleet. Together with Nos RT2819/3132, this bus has been re-engined with a Cummins B-series unit coupled to an Allison MT640 four-speed automatic gearbox*

alighting and boarding into and from the traffic lane, the two buses carried lady guards who, at each stop, would disembark and raise a red flag, halting following traffic, which would then wait until all passengers were clear before proceeding, and this feature of Unitrans operation continues right up to the present day.

If ASUCD had any misgivings about the wisdom of its decision, such doubt was dispelled quickly, the service being an immediate success, with the double-deckers proving to be the magnet that drew students out of their cars, and it was not all that long before other double-deckers were added, all ex-London stock but over a relatively long period of time. Interestingly, none of these subsequent buses were purchased from PVS, but were obtained from a variety of sources within the western USA, mostly from within California itself. Given the greater number built RTs of compared with RTLs, it was inevitable that further additions would be of AEC manufacture, and in 1970 came Nos RT1235 and 3123, the former carrying a Park Royal body, that on the latter being by Saunders but before arrival in Davis somewhere along the way the bus had lost its roofbox indicator.

In 1974, No RT3889 joined the fleet; in 1970 the bus had passed from the LTE to the-then newly-formed London Country Bus Services, being sold to Omnibus Promotions in 1973 and in June 1974 crossing the 'pond' to join ASUCD in the September. The next year saw No RT2819 at Davis, another PRV-bodied example; this had come via the unlikely route of a gentleman in Southall (of 'Windmill Lane' fame) and of an English pub in Santa Monica (your writer's previous California base), to arrive in northern California in December 1975. And as far as your writer is concerned, the 'prize' arrived at Davis in 1977.

While never making secret my distaste and loathing of the MCW Orion, at the same time I've been fairly vociferous in declaring my love for the RT-style roofbox (an abbreviation of the official 'Roof-Route-

Above: *The Sacramento dealer known formerly as Capital Bus sales is now Buy-a-Bus, and has two Bristol Lodekkas on its premises. One is an ex-Eastern National FLF6G, and the other, seen here, is an FSF6G, new to Midland General as No 504 in 1962, later passing to Trent.*

Right: *Some 90 miles west of Sacramento is San Francisco, with many transport attractions including the Gray Line fleet of Leyland Olympians with ECW bodies, owned by Grosvenor Bus Lines.*

Number-Box') body whether on an AEC or Leyland chassis, and No RT742 came attired with such, but there is an even greater personal link with this vehicle. In 1958 your scribe was in the midst of photographing as much London trolleybus fact as possible, knowing that within the shortness of time it would be but history. Unfortunately, this resulted in much of the LTE bus fleet being photographically ignored by M. J. Dryhurst and V. H. Darling *(thought by many to be one and the same person! Ed)*; on the one hand this was a somewhat disdainful stance born out of youthful arrogance ('well, it's just RF, RLH, RT, RTL RTW . . .') while on the other, the trolleybus end roller was already turning . . . Anyroad, for some extraordinary reason on one March day in 1958, MD was standing in the (trolleybus-less) Trafalgar Square when he espied nosing its way out of The Strand a roofbox RT on route 13; a quick adjustment to f5.6 @

1/100th immortalised the moment. The bus was RT742, carrying a Saunders body (albeit not the one fitted currently), and for some reason out of the thousands of bus shots I've taken since May 1950, this in particular is one that always has remained a favourite.

**Discovered in Hollywood**

I spent most of 1970 in Mexico . . . in the back-of-beyond Durango state, as the assistant director on the movie 'Lawman'; I made my way back to the UK via southern California, and one day I am walking down Cahuenga ('Car-weng-ah') Boulevard in downtown Hollywood, and there, standing beneath a high-rise building is a double-decker Brittanique. An RT, a roofbox RT . . . 742! The bus had been withdrawn from LTE stock in 1969 and sold to the London company Lex Garages Ltd; from there its history is vague, although less than a year later I found it sitting in

*While most of the ex-London buses in Unitrans' fleet carry 'London' destination details, the two ex-West Riding Daimler Fleetlines merely carry a fleetnumber in their destination screens. This is No 6773, formerly West Riding No 647, a 1969 Fleetline with Roe H77F body. Since purchase by Unitrans these buses have been fitted with a (US) nearside door and a wheelchair lift.*

'Tinseltown', in the ubiquitous 'USA LT Red' – which is a sort of faded burgundy into which colour were painted most ex-UK buses that were exported to North America. No RT742 came to the notice of ASUCD sometime in 1976, when it was owned by a realtor (estate agent) in the Bay Area (Greater San Francisco!) and then painted in what Unitrans general manager, James McElroy, described once as 'psychedelic puke'! The bus, roofbox and all, came to Davis in 1977.

There was then a lull in double-decker acquisitions but in 1979 came four such buses, the last serviceable ex-LTE stock. No RT3752 had been purchased by Omnibus Promotions of London, which company had Smith's of Reading convert it to a UK offside/US nearside entrance/exit; in this guise it went to a Thunderbird Red Lion Motor Inn at Jentzen Beach, Portland, Oregon. It turned-up at Davis in September

1979 but by October 1980 it had been stripped of all useful parts, being sold a year later. But its story doesn't end there. No RT4735 is the only Weymann-bodied bus left in the Unitrans fleet; withdrawn by LCBS in l972, it was sold then to a manufacturer of industrial coatings, which in turn sold it to Omnibus Promotions in June 1974. Five years later it turned up at Davis. In the fall of 1979 arrived two lowbridge buses, No RLH21/34. Freeway height restrictions precluded such RT-type running thereon so the RLH buses were bought with a view to generating private charter opportunities. But other events were afoot . . .

### Idiosyncrasies

It is one thing to bring-in secondhand foreign buses to operate intensive schedules; it is quite another to expect your indigenous maintenance staff to cope with them, their idiosyncrasies, their source of spares . . . gradually, the ex-LTE buses began to fail, being replaced by secondhand Flxible and GMC buses, so that by January 1984, none were serviceable, having been sidelined by the California highway patrol. Enter one Wally Mellor, an expatriate Brit from Liverpool ('The only good thing to come out of London was the M1!'). His background was as a driver in his father's road haulage business, and although a devotee of Leyland products, he is known to have a very soft spot for a certain AH470-engined AEC Mercury, but that is

Above: *Although all of the Flxible new-look buses have been withdrawn from the Unitrans fleet, a number of GM new-look buses survive. Seen in November 1997 is No 4508, a TDH-series 'fishbowl' wearing the earlier Unitrans livery.*

Right: *In addition to the Unitrans attractions there are other older vehicles at work within the Sacramento area. Although Amtrak, the federal railroad agency, requires bus lines to provide modern vehicles on sub-contracted services, Amador Stage Lines of Sacramento uses this mid-1970s GM P8M 4905A on frontline Amtrak work.*

the extent of his Southall accommodation. But Wally is a mechanical genius; Bill Cottrell and Tim Nicholson are others, as has to be Mike Sutcliffe. There has not been built an AEC, Gardner nor Leyland engine that Wally does not know his way around; there has not been built a GMC nor Cummins engine that Wally . . . etc, etc!

Wally arrived at Davis in January 1984. to find a very poor scene. While being a UK lorry devotee, he was very saddened by the sight of the discarded double-deckers and was determined to return them to a roadworthy and passenger-carrying state – if they were wanted.

They were. This situation was encouraged by James McElroy and also the Davis City Council, for as from 1974 the ASUCD services were restricted no longer to just students but served Davis citywide. Davis wanted

back its double-deckers, especially as they are great people-movers in the winter wet season, and Wally Mellor ensured they got them! But before Wally got to work, some changes had occurred to the ex-LTE fleet. Disposals had seen the demise of Nos RLH21/34, RT3572/3889 and RTL1194, plus the purchase of two Daimler Fleetline CRG6LX/Roe H77F ex-West Riding 647/8; of these disposals, No RT3889 emerged in the Los Angeles area while in late 1995, out of the blue, No RLH21 turned-up in south Sacramento County in the village of Sheldon, albeit wearing an RT radiator – shortly thereafter it was joined by ex-Unitrans No RT3752. Both buses are minus engine and gearbox, but they present a whole, while attention to the RT's paintwork can be detected. No RTL1194 suffered the same fate of running parts stripping and ended up in the eastern suburbs of Sacramento in a RV (Recreational Vehicle) park in Rancho Cordova; in

*Although Unitrans has only a full-time maintenance staff of seven, and no bodyshop or coachbuilding staff, it has built a new jic-wood roof for No RT1014 and completely rebuilt the body framework on Nos RT742, 3132 and 4735. Seen in December 1997, No RT3132 emerges from the Davis shop on its way to a local paintshop in neighbouring Dixon.*

late 1995 it disappeared from Rancho and neither has been seen nor heard of since, while a recent report suggests No RLH34 might be languishing in a tractor repair shop in Elk Grove, also on the south side of Sacramento. Your scribe is on the trail . . .

### Today's fleet

And what of the present-day Unitrans double-deck fleet? Apart from anything else, it is a testament to Jim McElroy, who is an advocate of those vehicles which can accommodate the highest passenger-carrying ability while occupying the least amount of roadspace – double-deckers. The City of Davis Council wants to see people out of cars and into buses by the most promising means – double-deckers. And Wally Mellor? He takes into account the prerequisites of his general manager, of ASCUD and his city, plus the fact that despite 20-plus years in the USA, he hasn't found a better bus than his RT family, currently sitting at five RTs and one RTL. Because of the parts problem, all of the AEC buses have been re-engined; Nos RT2819/3123/4735 all now boast Cummins B-series units coupled to Allison MT640 automatic gearboxes. No RT1235 carries a Leyland O.600 engine from Routemaster together with the original AEC transmission, while No RT742 recently had its AEC A204 engine replaced by an AEC 11.3-litre unit from a Militant, supplied by Don Allmey ('it goes like a tank', says Wally), this being done to retain its AEC pedigree.

No RTL1014 retains still the Leyland O.600 unit it had when it arrived in Davis over 30 years ago, but consideration is being given to giving it the Cummins treatment per the AECs. Despite the fact the Unitrans RT fleet is 45-50 years old, engines and transmissions

don't present the major headaches, but rear axles do. Wally Mellor cannot estimate how many gazzilion miles the rear axles have run, their differentials turned, and the problem with these units is that no company any longer produces a double-decker rear axle of 90in width; Wally feels confident that the necessary replacement parts could be manufactured in the Unitrans shop, if only he had a drawing of same. Answers please, on a postcard to Unitrans, that is U-N-I . . . And what of the two Fleetlines? Well, they are very popular and have proved worthy workhorses in the 16 years that they've been at Davis and there is a distinct possibility of them being replaced by lowfloor double-deckers, about which Wally has been talking to some firm in Guildford – but there are many bridges to cross yet, both on specifications and legal aspects.

One assumes that if you are reading this you are a devotee of the classic bus? Davis is but 75 miles east of San Francisco, 11 miles west of Sacramento. Besides its five RTs, one RTL and two Fleetlines, Unitrans includes also in its fleet such venerable US products as a 1958 GMC TDH3501 'old-look' plus late 1960s/early 1970s fishbowl 'new-looks', all well-maintained, all in everyday use and a testament to the operator and its dedicated maintenance staff. Oh, and yes, in case you're wondering – there is also a modern fleet of Unitrans buses, comprising Gillig Phantom and CNG-powered Orion Mk.V buses, these latter wearing a new Unitrans single-deck livery akin to the ex-LTE stock, which is painted LTE red with flake-grey relief, although No RT742 wears LTE 1948 red and cream colour scheme.

Just think, in a small, very accessible area of northern California you can see operating RT, RTL, CRG6, Eastern Coach Works-bodied three-axle Leyland Olympians, FLF Lodekkas, PCC streetcars and Blackpool 'boat' trams, plus at Woodland, Ca, is possibly the largest truck museum in the world. Come check us out . . . **CB**

*In conclusion, I acknowledge gratefully the assistance given by Unitrans general manager James McElroy and maintenance manager Wally Mellor, plus the use made of the PSV Circle/Omnibus Society publication PX3, 'Post War Second-Hand British Buses in North America'.*

*Michael Dryhurst spent the first 40 years of his working life in the movie industry, such work effecting a permanent move to the USA; having moved to Northern California, he is now the fleet manager of a limousine company. He has had published numerous books/articles on buses and trolleybuses, but still doesn't know what he wants to do when he grows up . . .*

# CHECKPOINT

## No2: Leyland Royal Tiger

**Born:** Leyland, Lancashire, April 1950.

**Main claim to fame:** First underfloor-engined Leyland chassis to go into volume production.

**Sounds like a lot of qualifications in that statement:** There are. In 1936/37, Leyland was enthused by American developments and was keenly interested in rear and underfloor-engined buses already running there. It brought a White underfloor-engined 'pancake' bus across the Atlantic, took it to bits and established how it could fit a horizontal Leyland diesel in place of the White petrol engine. By October 1937, the first of London Transport's 88 TF-class underfloor-engined Tigers had been built and, in May 1941, a solitary underfloor-engined six-wheel Panda was delivered to Alexander's in Scotland. Immediate postwar horizontal engine development was of an export version of the O.600 (the first of which, ominously as fate would later have it, went to Scania) and of the chassisless Olympic which was marketed jointly with MCW and announced at the end of 1949.

**Why underfloor engines, anyway?:** Above all, because the absence of engine intrusion made space for seats. It also was believed that they had better weight distribution and were cheaper to run.

**So why develop the Royal Tiger?:** Largely to meet demand for products that didn't have MCW bodies, and especially to offer an underfloor-engined coach. As Leyland had bypassed its own coachworks to tie up the deal with MCW on the Olympic, it was able to resume single-deck bodybuilding in 1950 after a space of 11 years when military and double-deck production had taken precedence. A fondly remembered, if ever-so-slightly old fashioned-looking centre-entrance coach body was offered first, followed in 1951 by a bus version with flat front and entrance.

**It came in how many forms?:** Eight to start with, conveniently designated PSU1/1 to 8. All were to be 27ft 6in long, the first four being 7ft 6in wide, the second four 8ft wide. The odd-numbered models had vacuum brakes and the evens had air brakes, while models PSU1/3, 4, 7 and 8 nominally were the coach versions with a drop-frame chassis extension behind the back axle to make space for a boot. But events got in the way of these models ever appearing.

**Come again:** Construction & Use regulations changed in 1950 to permit 30ft two-axle single-deckers, so PSU1/1 to 8 were replaced by 30ft PSU1/9 to 16. An 8ft wide, vacuum-braked bus chassis, PSU1/17, joined them in 1951. Oh, and PSU appears to have stood for Passenger Single-deck Underfloor (or, Leyland expert Doug Jack speculates, maybe Underslung). For overseas markets, there were models of up to 35ft 6in designated OPSU1, 2 and 3 which were not to be confused with the PSU3 Leopard of the 1960s and 1970s. At this stage, all models had synchromesh gearboxes.

**And you got MCW bodies on the Olympic and Leyland on the Royal Tiger?:** Yes, but more besides including, incorrigibly, MCW-bodied Royal Tigers. Alexander, Saunders Roe, Burlingham, Duple, Brush, Windover, Bellhouse-Hartwell and ECW all did their bit, too.

**ECW?:** Nineteen buses and coaches for United and Cumberland were delivered in 1951 and 1953 to styles normally associated with the Bristol LS. The chassis came from unbreakable pre-nationalisation orders placed by Cumberland.

**Sounds like it was a rip-roaring success:** To begin with, it

was. But as postwar realities of rising costs and free-falling patronage began to eat into operators' profits, the Royal Tiger started to look a tad too heavy. Experience would prove that it was built to last and that it probably made a good long-term investment, but things didn't look that way by 1952 when two tons were shaved out of body and chassis to create the Tiger Cub. We were entering an age of lean engineering rather than the generous over-engineering that begat the Royal Tiger.

**And that was the end of the Royal Tiger?:** It was the end of its home market pre-eminence, but it lived on as an export product, including Royal Holland integrals for, one need hardly say, the Netherlands. After over 6,000 were built, production ended in 1955, replaced by the Royal Tiger Worldmaster, an 8ft wide air-braked model with Pneumo-cyclic semi-automatic gearbox and a choice of O.600 or O.680 horizontal engines and a range of wheelbases allowing bodywork up to 37ft. It was introduced in 1954 and was intended as a home and export model, but British length limits meant only two models, the RT3/1 bus and RT3/2 coach, could be sold here.

**And were they?:** The coach sold in penny numbers, while 39 Weymann-bodied RT3/1s went to Glasgow and Halifax which, by some happy coincidence, both painted their buses in the same green, cream and orange colours which the latter copied from the former after borrowing a manufacturers' prewar demonstrator in Glasgow livery. These Worldmasters – Leyland eventually stopped using the Royal Tiger name – were delivered between 1956 and 1958 and the Glasgow machines proved to live up to their name by venturing well beyond their home city.

**To where?:** Southend and central Scotland to start with, then Australia where three surplus chassis fetched up in the early 1970s, with at least one being lengthened before being rebodied. Another that stayed put in Britain was given a newer Plaxton coach body.

**And the Worldmaster itself?:** The home market model was finally dropped from Leyland's options in 1964, but exports continued well into the early-1970s. Twenty-three very impressive Ogle-designed 40-seaters were built for CIE's touring fleet in Ireland in 1962-4, but serious problems led to them being rebodied by Van Hool in 1970; the chassis were as good as any Royal Tiger derivative – these were ERT2/1s – and some survived until very recently with Bus Eireann.

**And that was it?:** Not quite. From 1962 to 1968, Leyland sold a contraption called the Royal Tiger Cub which, to simplify descriptions, was a beefed-up 33ft Leopard. It sold about 600, mostly for export, but Doncaster Corporation took 20 with Roe bodies in 1965 and 1968. **ALM**

The existence of the Leyland-MCW Olympic didn't discourage operators from choosing Royal Tigers with Weymann bodywork, like this East Yorkshire PSU1/13 with rear entrance, seen in York in 1959.
Michael Dryhurst

# BEFORE & AFTER

R. D. OKILL was one of that pioneering band of bus photographers who captured some prewar and early postwar gems on film. This selection covers coaches and buses before World War 2 on the Isle of Wight and after the War in Cornwall

The proximity of the Isle of Wight to the south coast meant that it was a popular destination for holidaymakers in the prewar days, and this led to the growth of a number of private coach operators. The Isle of Wight photos were all taken in the summer of 1938. Pink Bros DL 9661 was a Dennis Lancet with centre entrance Dennis coach bodywork.

On a tour from the mainland, Hants & Dorset No F488, a 1935 Leyland Tiger TS7 with Beadle bodywork.

A fine normal control Dennis Lancet with Duple coach body,
DL 8494 in the fleet of Moss Motor Tours of Sandown.

Rear views from this period are rare. This shows the tail of the
same coach, Moss Motor Tours DL 8494.

*Eames Tours of Shanklin operated yet another Dennis Lancet,*
*ADL 401 with Harrington coachwork, No 12 in the fleet.*

*The stylish rear of a similar Eames coach, ADL 629.*

*At Newquay in 1947, Western National No 509, a Bedford OWB with utility Duple 32-seat bodywork.*

*At The Moor, Falmouth, in 1952, Western National No 209, a Bristol JO5G with replacement Beadle rear entrance 36-seat bus body.*

*The Moor, Falmouth pictured again in 1952, with Western National No 629, a Dennis Mace with 26-seat Bristol body.*

*At Lynmouth in 1946, Western National No 411, a Bedford WLB with 25-seat Duple body.*

*Rather newer Western National fare, Bristol LS6G No 1359 with ECW 41-seat coach body, at Perranporth in 1956.*

*Minehead in 1946 and a Blue Motors (Porlock Weir, Porlock & Minehead Service Co Ltd) Leyland Lion LT7 with front-entrance Harrington coachwork.*

# JUST A HANDFUL

## P. R. WALLIS looks back at privately-operated bus services in postwar London

*The signwriting on the side of this ex-Tynemouth AEC Regent II/Weymann proclaims 'This would not be the only bus running in London if there had been a secret ballot of the busmen'. It is seen pulling away from the Marble Arch stop in London's Oxford Street in the summer of 1958 while being 'operated' by the People's League for the Defence of Freedom during the infamous London bus strike at that time.*
Michael Dryhurst

*For some time the normal vehicle used on Continental Pioneer's 235 Richmond local service was this ex-Thames Valley Bristol LWL6B with ECW body, seen here turning at Friar's Stile Road.*
Michael Dryhurst

W ITH THE completion of the privatisation of the London Buses operating companies, it is interesting to look back to a period when privately-operated bus services were very much the exception in the London area.

The formation of London Passenger Transport Board in July 1933 created a monopoly area for London Transport buses within an approximate 25-mile radius of the capital. All bus services operating wholly within that area were compulsorily acquired by London Transport who then divided operations into the well known Central Area (red buses) and Country Area (green buses).

The monopoly position continued well into postwar days. True, provincial buses were to be seen in the capital during some of the darkest days of World War 2, and in the late 1940s the Tilling group sent many new Bristol K types to London; at around the same time London Transport hired up to 535 coaches, mostly from London coach operators. But all these vehicles were hired by London Transport to cover acute vehicle shortages at those times. They worked London Transport services under that organisation's full control.

### Flexibility

It was in the mid-1950s that the first hint of some small degree of flexibility emanated from 55 Broadway. London Transport announced that it would be willing to help any small firms willing to tackle any of the shorter, more local routes. This came at a time when most bus operators were starting to notice the decline in passenger loadings from the early postwar highs, and doubtless London Transport was seeking to make economies.

Some local coach operators responded to this initiative and amongst those who provided services were Banstead Coaches (Banstead-Chipstead Valley, and Coulsdon-Woodcote), Brownes Transport (Redhill-Horley), Falcon Coaches (Hampton-Hanworth), Sunnymede (Grange Hill-Chigwell Row),

*Continental Pioneer also used ex-London buses like the former RF258, seen at Richmond station in June 1970, although this bus returned to the London area after a stint with Premier Travel, Cambridge.*
P. R. Wallis

and West London Coachways (Feltham-Bedfont).

It has to be remembered that these routes were marginal in terms of distance and represented an infinitesimally small proportion of London Transport's total mileage.

For instance the Feltham-Bedfont service of West London Coachways, started on 7 October 1955, was just over a mile in length with a six-minute journey time. Nevertheless this service, along roads not previously covered by London Transport, met a demand and it prospered, eventually being acquired in January 1967 by Golden Miller Coaches of Feltham.

### Emergency situation

In 1958 a variety of independent services were to be seen in London for a very brief period. A strike by crews caused the complete withdrawal of all London Transport road services from 5 May to 20 June that year. In the emergency situation the London Transport Executive granted licences for a number of stage carriage services.

The most prominent operator was an organisation called The People's League for the Defence of Freedom which was granted licences for these services:

1  Victoria-Marble Arch

2  Addington-Croydon

3  Barnes-Roehampton

5  Archway-Friern Barnet

6  Oval-Thornton Heath

7  Surbiton-Richmond

8  Woolwich-Chislehurst

The League assembled a motley collection of fascinating vehicles from London dealers which were then pressed into service. These included, inter alia, two ex-Leicester AEC Renown six-wheelers (believed to have been the last time this model was used in passenger service), ex-East Kent Leyland Tiger TS8 coaches and ex-Crosville Leyland Titan TD7s.

Above: **Elms of Kenton used this former United Bristol LS/ECW bus on the 98B service. It is seen in a typical suburban setting in Ruislip in November 1971.**
P. R. Wallis

Below: **Thames Weald used this Bedford VAS1/Plaxton on its service from Romford to Sevenoaks, through the Dartford Tunnel. It is seen at Dartford in May 1970, with RT3016 passing on the 96.**
P. R. Wallis

Golden Miller used a variety of new and secondhand vehicles on its services in southwest London. A 1950 ex-Thames Valley Bristol LL5G/ECW, rebuilt with a full front, is seen in High Street, Feltham in July 1970.
T. Wright

A Golden Miller AEC Reliance/Roe, ex-Doncaster Corporation, at Ashford Common in September 1971.
T. Wright

Licences were also granted to some independent operators, although not all services granted a licence actually ran. Amongst those that did operate were Chiltern Queens, which ran a service from Chiswick to Hyde Park Corner, and Edward Thomas of Ewell, which operated from Chessington to Richmond.

Poor industrial relations – during the period, a persistent feature of not just the bus industry but of much British industry generally – led to the next flowering of independent services in London.

### Short-lived

Central Area crews imposed a rest day and overtime working ban which led the London Transport Board to withdraw a number of services from 30 January 1966. As a result the Board issued emergency licences to independent operators to cover around 30 London Transport services. Many of these independent operations were short-lived as the Board later restored workings to a number of the withdrawn services. However, a few of the withdrawn services were destined to become regular operations by independent concerns.

Of these, one of the shortest routes in terms of distance was the 235 which Isleworth Coaches took over on 31 January 1966. The route linked Richmond with Richmond Hill, a distance of about a mile and the journey time was six minutes. Perhaps the

Two ex-Portsmouth Leyland Tiger Cubs with MCW bodies rest at Bedfont Lane bus station, Feltham, on Golden Miller's 604 and 601 services.
T. Wright

Golden Miller bought three of these Bedford YRQ with Plaxton 37-seat bodies in 1974. SYO 600N is seen at Stanwell in September 1974.
T. Wright

steepness of Richmond Hill encouraged patronage, in any event the service survived and passed in 1968 to Continental Pioneer who often used ex-London RFs and RTLs on it.

By contrast, another independently-operated route to emerge in 1966 was much longer. Route 98B operated in the northwestern suburbs of London linking Rayners Lane station with Ruislip station via Pinner with a through journey time of 38 minutes. Following

unsuccessful attempts by Worldwide Coaches and Valliant-Cronshaw to run part, or all, of the service it was taken over by Elms Coaches of Kenton on 1 August 1966. The difficulties must have been considerable bearing in mind the lapses in regular service over several months. Initially operation was by ex-Maidstone & District Commer/Harrington Contenders but later Bristol LS types became regular vehicles.

As mentioned earlier, Golden Miller acquired the

*This former Glasgow Corporation Leyland Atlantean/Alexander was one of two double-deckers bought by Golden Miller for school contracts, and is seen at Stanwell in December 1976.*
T. Wright

*Two of the Leyland Panther Cubs bought by Manchester Corporation found their way quickly into the Golden Miller fleet. BND 876C and BND 868C meet at Feltham station in July 1972.*
T. Wright

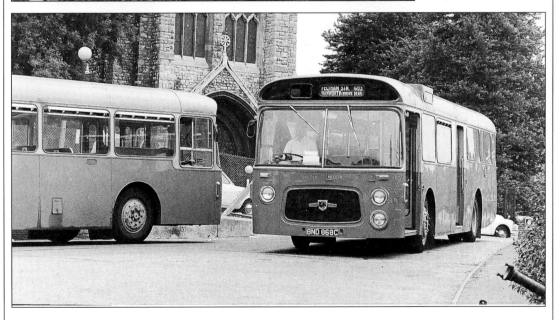

West London Coachways' Feltham-Bedfont service in 1967. Golden Miller then went on to develop a bit of a network in southwest London, providing links from Feltham to Shepperton, Hanworth and Walton-on-Thames as well as a service between Staines and Stanwell which Tellings-Golden Miller continued to operate until 1996 when the service was acquired by London & Country.

**Considerable network**

Other important independent services were developed on the southern and eastern sides of London. North Downs Rural Transport built up a considerable network based on Orpington, including a link to Croydon.

Super Coaches of Upminster, starting in 1960, linked housing developments with rail stations in its

An ex-Hants & Dorset Bristol RELL/ECW on Golden Miller's 601 service passes London Transport Leyland National LS31 on the 116 at Bedfont Green in March 1986.
T. Wright

TUR 347E, a Ford R192/Strachan new in 1967 to Knight, Hemel Hempstead, and acquired by Golden Miller the following year. It is seen at Feltham station in June 1970.
P. R. Wallis

area. Thames Weald's link through the Dartford Tunnel came about and continues to this day.

All these services met a need and to the enthusiast provided a welcome variety in terms of vehicle types and liveries against what was at the time a highly-standardised London Transport scenario. It should not be forgotten that all the services referred to could only be operated with London Transport's permission, perhaps not so different from today when the privatised operators still have to obtain a franchise for a route from London Transport Buses. **CB**

*Philip Wallis lived in Baughurst, Hampshire, close to a small Venture depot, where a friendly staff helped him to become a bus enthusiast at the age of four. Following schooldays he undertook engineering training at Thornycroft in Basingstoke, followed by a period of commissioned service in the Royal Engineers. Since that time he has worked in sales and executive capacities in the construction plant and agricultural machinery industries. He has always maintained a strong interest in the bus industry and is a keen bus photographer.*

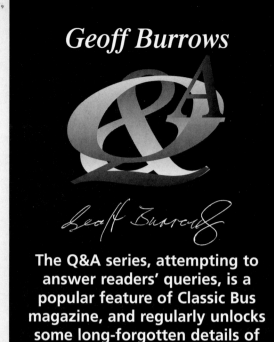

# Geoff Burrows

*Geoff Burrows* (signature)

The Q&A series, attempting to answer readers' queries, is a popular feature of Classic Bus magazine, and regularly unlocks some long-forgotten details of buses and bus companies

## COLOUR MATCHING

*Q In CB29 we published an article about Bamber Bridge Motor Services, and showed a photograph of 'the famous Albion demonstrator 747 EUS . . . being new in February 1963'. Alistair Ramsay writes from Newton Mearns to say that in 'Glasgow's Trams and Buses', by Robert Grieves there is a photograph of 747 on trial in Glasgow during 1962 in full GCT livery. Alistair wants to know what the correct date was when the vehicle was new.*

*A* The Albion Lowlander mentioned was actually first seen at the Scottish Motor Exhibition, Kelvin Hall, Glasgow in November 1961. It was in full GCT livery but without any registration number. It worked for Glasgow from Newlands garage for nearly a year, starting in March 1962. It was then re-painted red and white and spent six months on demonstration to Edinburgh. Neither undertaking followed up the trials with orders, and the vehicle was eventually owned by Bamber Bridge. It is of interest to note in passing that three years later Edinburgh conducted more new bus trials. One of the vehicles involved was the rather similar AEC Renown, it too received no orders.

## JUNKERS GROUNDED

*Q Many trade magazines produce, from time to time, data books of facts and figures collated from the best information available at that time. Andrew Emmerson of Northampton has been reading one such book from about 1931, 'Compression Ignition Engines for Road Vehicles'. Included in an extremely dull article about fuel oil viscosity and flash point, is a photograph of a bus captioned 'A Junkers-type double-crankshaft oil engine is employed in this ultra-modern front-wheel-drive Gilford double-decker'. This has aroused Andrew's interest, and he would be fascinated to know more.*

*A* Andrew's picture shows the revolutionary Gilford low-height double decker, the subject of Alan Millar's 'Classic Blunderbus' in CB4. It was shown in the 1931 Commercial Motor Show; the engine was in fact a wooden dummy, since Gilford and Junkers had 'contractual difficulties'. The engine

and transmission was all up at the front, allowing a very low floor indeed, the overall height being only 12ft 11in (about 3.9m). Turbo-charging was proposed, but the blower would have been only half a metre from the drivers ear in an enclosed cab! There are many contradictions about the design, but since all the drawings and the vehicles (yes-vehicles plural – there was also a single-decker) were destroyed, we will probably never know all the details. The single decker did run as a test vehicle, probably fitted with either an AEC or a Meadows engine. The double-decker was converted with an electric motor to become a trolleybus. As such it ran for a while at Wolverhampton, but the project was already in jeopardy due to the poor financial health of the Gilford company. R. D. Okill, who has researched the project, wrote in 1983, 'Little remains but the mystery'.

## RAIL-LESS

*Q 'How many buses did British Railways own and operate, what did they use them for, and where and when?', asks David Thrower of Warrington.*

*A* Fortunately, that question was at the end of David's very interesting letter. If it had been at the beginning, we would have panicked! He writes to say that he owns an ex-BR Bristol L, ex-Lincolnshire, and he has found a photograph of an ex-NGT Guy Arab in British Railways red/cream livery. So we know that he is talking about the first 20 years or so of BR, when the years of neglect due to the war had to be put right. BR used the buses to transport the teams of skilled men directly from main centres such as Newcastle to the many outlying areas which were difficult to reach (even by train). Large numbers of buses were obtained all over the country for this work, many of them Gardner-engined for reliability. By the 1970s BR was buying new vehicles for this work, which of course was now normal maintenance and repair. The new vehicles were to its own design, built on lorry chassis such as Bedford or BMC, and were effectively large 'crew-cab' arrangements, sometimes combined with a mobile workshop. Their successors can be seen at work today. We have no doubt that some of our readers have studied this interesting subject, and we look forward to their comments. For the record, about 11 Guy Arabs from the Northern General fleet finished up with BR.

## DESTINATION UNKNOWN

*Q 'Who was the first British manufacturer or operator to introduce fabric destination blinds, and who first lit them from behind?', asks Ian Reid of Swanley. He also wants to know who first had electronic indicators, as well as dates for all these events.*

*A* Linen blinds, with lighting and roller mechanisms were in use in the last decade of the last century, on trams in the USA. They were therefore in use before the first motorbuses. They became common, though not universal, on the early electric trams in this country, usually made or supplied by the tram builders themselves. Consequently the very early buses could have had them, but many operators would have thought them an unnecessary expense. In fact painted boards, 'tin-bibles' and stencils were in use in many fleets until quite recently and paper slips are still stuck into front windows, mainly north of the border. One of the earliest blind manufacturers that we know of was Gawthorpe & Co. of Leeds, and the Equipment Engineering Co. made winding mechanisms. Trials with electronic indicators were made during the 1970s, without much success. However, the first commercially successful type was introduced at the 1980 Motor Show at the NEC. The Luminator electronic indicator display was fitted to several vehicles, including a Northern Counties Olympian for Greater Manchester, and an Alexander Olympian for Strathclyde.

# EARLY SMALL DIESEL BUSES

## ALAN TOWNSIN reflects on some revealing statistics which bring to light an unsung if small-scale Leyland sales success story

*London Transport's territory as originally constituted included some surprisingly rural backwaters. For routes in such areas, 74 Leyland Cub KPO3 20-seat buses with Short Bros bodywork were placed in service in spring 1935, the first large order for small diesel buses in Britain and, as it turned out, set to remain unsurpassed in numbers until the 1950s. Seen on the 450 route linking Dartford and Gravesend via local villages is No C69.*

FIGURES relating to the quantities of the nation's stock of buses are usually so large as to seem difficult to relate to specific vehicles. Yet by looking at the totals for some individual groups, a clearer picture emerges.

Recently the editor sent me some photocopies of various articles in the monthly magazine *Bus & Coach* dating from the 1930s. Among them were commentaries on annual Ministry of Transport statistics by Irwin Jeffery, drawing attention to some significant trends. That decade was one of immense change, including a strong upsurge in the total numbers of diesel buses.

In those days, figures were recorded for the numbers of public service vehicles (the generic term used in official circles for buses and coaches licensed to carry the public), covering both the totals in use and the new vehicles registered during each year ending 30 September. They were split into seating capacity groups – 9-20, 21-26, 27-32, 33-48, and over 48. Incidentally these groups were largely as used in setting the licence fees, which accounts for why seating capacities of say 27 or 33 were so rare in those days – after the war a new system applied with rates more directly related to the actual figure.

The figures reproduced were split, at least for some periods, so as to record petrol and diesel (in those days often described as oil-engined) vehicles separately and in some cases the numbers then become small enough to allow a process of recollection and a bit of delving to bring the dry figures to life.

The diesel psv was by then just beginning to become well established in Britain in 1934, with a total of 2,398 examples of all sizes in use out of the overall total of 44,677 motor buses and coaches at 30 September – admittedly only a little over 5%, but growing rapidly, especially among double-deckers where the proportion had already reached about twice that figure.

*The prototype for London Transport's fleet of Leyland Cub buses, built in June 1934 and numbered C1, was petrol-engined as built, still being so in this scene at Sunbury Cross in November of that year, but in June 1935 it received a Perkins four-cylinder diesel engine, running thus until it became petrol again in 1939. The body was built in the LPTB workshops at Chiswick.*

The total numbers of new diesel buses in the 9-20-seat and 21-26-seat classes recorded in Great Britain for successive years in the mid-1930s were smaller than I had realised, running as follows (I have included new petrol equivalents for comparison):

*Crosville Motor Services Ltd was the largest user of Leyland Cub buses of the various types built in the 1930s, with a total of 165, using them largely in rural areas of north Wales, but most of them were petrol-engined. Many had entered service before the diesel version became available, as applied to this 1933 KP2, one of six with 20-seat body by Chas T. W. Tooth, a Wrexham firm which supplied similar bodies on six 1KPO2 oil-engined chassis in 1935 – most Crosville Cubs had bodies by Brush or Weymann.*

| | NEW VEHICLES | | | | VEHICLES IN USE | |
|---|---|---|---|---|---|---|
| | 9-20 seats | | 21-26 seats | | 9-20 seats | 21-26 seats |
| Year ended 30 Sept | Petrol | Oil | Petrol | Oil | Oil | Oil |
| 1934 | 688 | - | 107 | - | 16 | 70 |
| 1935 | 520 | 83 | 267 | 20 | 117 | 65 |
| 1936 | 454 | 33 | 459 | 7 | 143 | 53 |
| 1937 | 283 | 39 | 640 | 28 | 182 | 78 |
| 1938 | 222 | 27 | 706 | 13 | 206 | 90 |

Note that the total number of existing diesel-engined vehicles in use in the small 9-20-seat class at 30 September 1934 was only 16, out of a total of 9,617 vehicles of this seating capacity range, or fewer than two in every thousand. Even by 1938, the figure of those in use had risen only to 206 out of 6,464, just over 3% whereas by then among buses seating over 48 (all double-deck in those days) diesels had reached 62%.

The small bus or coach of any type was becoming considerably less numerous than it had been. In 1926, the 9-20-seat class had amounted to 20,229 vehicles, which represented the remarkable proportion of just over half the 40,118 total of all psvs and trolleybuses (the latter few in number at that date but included in the recorded totals – so far as I know, there were no trolleybuses in the up-to-26-seat classes). The 9-20-seat total fell slightly up to 1930, when it was 19,199, but then very sharply to 14,298 in 1931, suggesting that the new vehicle certifying system introduced under the Road Traffic Act 1930 may have weeded out many sub-standard small buses. The fall then continued at a slightly less dramatic rate, the 9,617 figure of 1934 dropping to 6,464 by 1938.

In passing, it is significant that in the 1920s, which could be regarded as almost 'deregulated', small buses

This Leyland Cub KP3 demonstrator with Park Royal 26-seat body built to Southampton Corporation requirements was registered in Surrey as CPC 717 by Leyland's Kingston-on-Thames works. It was placed in service early in 1935, initially on loan, and 11 further buses with basically similar bodywork ordered for delivery later that year. These latter were oil-engined, but two more Cubs supplied in 1939 were petrol. Permission was obtained for the 26-seat buses to be operated without conductors, as sometimes given elsewhere – the general limit in those days was 20 seats.

were in such widespread favour, most of them run by small concerns or individuals. Some larger operators operated limited numbers of such buses, sometimes as 'chasers' to combat competition, but the major fleets favoured larger buses. In those days there was no general route licensing system, such control as there was being imposed by a system of local authority licensing which was at most patchy in effect. In the aftermath of World War 1, many ex-servicemen who had gained experience with motor vehicles and low-priced models such as the Ford Model T or other small types were the foundation of many an independent business. The decline in small vehicles continued in the 1930s – economics were making them less attractive, despite the fact that in those days they were the only type not needing a conductor when in use as buses.

The 21-26-seat class had been less numerous in the 1920s but climbed in numbers from 1926, when it was 4,027, to peak at 6,649 in 1930 and then sank again but more slowly, dropping back to 4,078 in 1938, almost back to the 1926 figure though levelling out latterly. Here the history was a little different, since the 26-seat size had implied a full-sized bonneted single-decker bus in the mid-1920s in quite a high proportion of fleets. Another factor had been the popularity of this capacity for coaches, either bonneted or even forward-control, the latter often with two-door layout. The numbers tended to fall in the early 1930s as these were scrapped (or in some cases, where coaches were reseated with higher capacities for use as buses), yet being counterbalanced towards the end of the period by the growing popularity of a new generation of lighter vehicle in the 25- or 26-seat class, most notably the Bedford.

The average seating capacity of all vehicles rose from 30.89 in 1931 to 35.05 in 1937. As judged 60 years later this latter once again seems a reasonable-sounding sort of figure, evoking a mental picture of a modern Dennis Dart or the like, so to some degree history has repeated itself.

### The advent of the small diesel

Back in the early 1930s, the build-up of knowledge on diesel engine design was such that developing engines suitable for smaller vehicles was still pushing at the frontiers of technology. Experimental operation of oil-engined buses of any size in public service in Britain had not begun until 1930. Most early road-vehicle diesel engines had cylinders of not much less than 1.4-litre capacity; hence four cylinders, generally agreed as the minimum for acceptable smoothness, implied 5.6 litres, too big for a small bus.

A list published in *The Commercial Motor* in May 1933 quoted only four oil engines (as they were then often called) on the British market with capacity of less than 5 litres – the Dorman 4JUR of 4.2 litres, the

Mercedes-Benz OM59 of 3.76 litres, the Perkins PL4 of 2.9 litres, all with four cylinders, and the Petter ACE3 of 4.2 litres, which was a three-cylinder two-stroke. In practice, of these only the Dorman 4JUR seems to have been used in any serious quantity in British buses (being favoured by W. Alexander & Sons to convert quite a number of its Albion 30/60hp models), though in later years Perkins became the main proprietary maker of small diesels for road transport use.

The bare statistics do sometimes hide the inclusion of vehicles other than the lighter types usually in mind when seating capacity of 26 or less is mentioned in the context of the 1930s. In the summer of 1934, Burton-on-Trent Corporation placed four new oil-engined 26-seat buses in service on heavy-duty bonneted chassis – two Guy Arab with Gardner 4LW engines, one AEC Ranger and one Leyland Lioness LTB, the latter two the only four-cylinder examples of their respective types. Yet this was really a rare throwback to an earlier era, the Burton undertaking being very conservative in its choice of vehicle layout at the time. Another quite different group of vehicles which confused the issue in statistical terms were six luxurious Leyland Tiger TS7 oil-engined coaches placed in service on its Edinburgh-London service by SMT in July 1936, for they seated only 22 passengers. There were other groups of special-purpose large small-capacity coaches in various fleets, but at that date petrol engines were still usual for such vehicles.

In practice, it was Leyland that was the first maker to obtain substantial orders for small oil-engined buses and by far the most successful in this limited category in the mid-1930s. A 4.4-litre six-cylinder oil engine for the lightweight Cub range had been announced later in 1933, its cylinder dimensions being the same as used for the petrol version, though the engine design was quite different, including the use of overhead valves instead of the side valves of the petrol unit and a scaled-down version of the pot-cavity direct-injection system used on the larger Leyland oil engines of the day.

It seems to have taken a little time to get into production but sales then got off to a good start with an order placed in August 1934 from London Transport for 74 Cub KPO3 buses with 20-seat bodywork by Short Bros, painted green for use on rural routes – in those days the area covered extended well into the countryside. They were placed in service in spring 1935, numbered C2-75, and conformed to that undertaking's declared policy of standardising on oil-engined buses, though No C1, the prototype completed in 1934, had been petrol.

Also in 1935, a batch of 12 oil-engined Cubs was supplied to Crosville Motor Services Ltd, already a major user of the petrol version. These are recorded as being of type 1KPO2, having 20-seat bodywork, this part of the order being split between Tooth, a Wrexham-based firm, and Brush.

The KPO3 had a longer wheelbase than usually regarded as necessary for 20-seat bodywork, though London Transport had chosen it in the interest of comfort. There were 11 more examples of the model which entered service with Southampton Corporation in August-September 1935, all but two with 26-seat capacity. The exceptions had 20 coach seats and rear luggage compartments for use in connection with Jersey Airways flights from Southampton airport.

## Revised designations

The story for 1936 was not dissimilar. Coventry Corporation placed three Leyland Cub 1KPO2 buses with Brush 20-seat bodywork in service early in the year. London Transport took delivery of a further 22 oil-engined 20-seat Cubs (Nos C77-98), of similar style to their predecessors but this time for central area services and having Weymann-built bodywork on KPZO2 chassis. Leyland's designations had been revised and the '2' suffix now indicated the longer 15ft 6in wheelbase previously indicated by '3'.

By then the Cub engine size had risen to 4.7-litres, the diesel version switching to indirect injection, an early example of this engine having been fitted to No C51 of the previous batch in November 1935 and it has been reported that the 11 buses for Southampton also had this engine. Another, smaller-scale, diesel Cub user was Swindon Corporation, which took four KPZO2 models in the summer to autumn of 1936 but these had larger-capacity bodywork by Weymann, thought to seat 24.

Crosville seems not to have been convinced of the merits of the diesel Cub on the evidence of its first examples, its 1936 Cub deliveries reverting to being petrol-engined, but in the earlier part of 1937 there were further oil-engined batches, of 12 KPZO1 (14ft wheelbase) and 10 of the KPZO2, all bodied by Brush with 20- and 26-seat capacities respectively. In truth, neither Cub diesel seems to have been very successful, less so than the petrol units found in most Crosville Cubs and used exclusively in several other fleets of the model, even where diesels had become standard for larger buses. On the other hand, London Transport was thinking of rebodying its Cubs in 1950 until it became known that Leyland was soon to stop making spares for the model.

However, a major new user for the oil-engined Cub, following delivery of a petrol batch in 1936, was the Lincolnshire Road Car Co Ltd, which took 30 KPZO1 in 1937 and 20 in 1938, all but two having 20-seat bus bodies by Brush, the exceptions having Duple coach bodies, also 20-seat.

London Transport had one further diesel Cub in the period under review, this being the prototype rear-engined example No CR1, of which the chassis was delivered in October 1937. Rather surprisingly at that date, it had the earlier 4.4-litre direct-injection engine, perhaps on the basis of standardisation with the country area Cubs. The 20-seat body built by LPTB itself was fitted just before the end of the year and it entered service in the Country Area. A production batch of 49 vehicles, of generally similar design but with indirect-injection engines, was not completed until after war broke out in September 1939.

Leyland didn't quite have it all its own way in the small diesel bus class at that time, even though most other makers did not even list vehicles in this class among their standard products. Even as late as November 1936, the only other maker offering small diesel models in a list quoted in *Motor Transport* was Commer. Its PN4 and PNF4 models, respectively quoted as of 20- and 26-seat size were available with an engine identifiable as the Perkins four-cylinder 3.99-litre Leopard, but in practice such vehicles were very rare indeed among the quite sizeable numbers of Commer coaches with the side-valve six-cylinder petrol engine, basically as used in Humber cars of the day and almost all sold to independent operators.

## Rare option

The official Society of Motor Manufacturers and Traders list of November 1937 went slightly further in mentioning that the Albion Victor PH/PK 114/115 and Guy Wolf CF20 and rather larger Vixen were available with oil engines (of unspecified type, though Albion had fitted Dorman engines in some export Victors) in addition to the petrol units listed – by then the larger Commer was the PLNF5, available with the Perkins Leopard II, still four-cylinder but of 4.4-litre capacity and equally rare with this option. The Albion Victor was quite a popular model but almost all those of that period had four-cylinder petrol engines as built, while the small Guy passenger models of that era were built only in very limited numbers, again almost all petrol.

None of the small diesel buses were anywhere near as numerous as the main petrol models in this size range. By far the most popular type in the 26-seat class being placed in service from late 1935, greatly outnumbering all other models, was the Bedford WTB and that was offered only in petrol form, as was the similarly popular previous WLB 20-seat model and indeed all Bedford models until well after World War 2. The sheer value offered by the WTB with its smooth-running standard 3.18-litre (3.5-litre from 1938) six-cylinder petrol engine was so overwhelming as to make competition with dearer models very difficult. In November 1937, the WTB chassis price was a mere £290, when the oil-engined Cub range began at £735 (£580 upwards for a petrol version), and even the very basic Commer PN3 with four-cylinder Perkins diesel was £467.

Dennis had quite an important share of the small bus market, notably with the Ace 20-seater apt to be better known by its nickname 'The Flying Pig', which was quite widely favoured by major as well as smaller operators especially in the 1934-6 period. Almost all of these had the standard 3.77-litre four-cylinder petrol engine, and such a chassis was £395 in 1937 – good value for quite a high-quality if simple product but still no match for the Bedford in sales appeal to most operators.

However, almost at the end of Ace production, and indeed after the model was no longer generally listed, the Eastern Counties Omnibus Co Ltd had some batches of 20-seat buses on a modified version of this chassis with the Gardner 4LK engine. This latter, introduced in 1935, shared the Gardner reputation for efficiency with its larger brethren, scaled down to 3.8-litre capacity. It was quite widely used in goods vehicles but was rare in buses until some time later, most notably the lightweight Bristol SC4LK 35-seater of the mid-1950s which produced almost legendary fuel consumption figures of 20mpg or so. The first batch of eight Dennis Ace 4LK-powered models for Eastern Counties entered service in the spring of 1938. Twelve more were built in 1939-40.

Just how far the above-mentioned batches of vehicles dominated the deliveries of new small diesel buses can be seen from the following. In 1937 and 1938 there appear to have been more vehicles in the 9-20-seat class supplied than were recorded nationally. Just possibly, this may have been because of some vehicles delayed in delivery or not licensed immediately, but the possibility of clerical error does seem to arise.

The identity of the vehicles not specified, more especially among the 21-26-seat category, is a matter for some speculation and the author would welcome information on any not mentioned. Some may have been diesel examples of the Commer, Albion or Guy models quoted above, or further diesel Cubs, perhaps sold to small operators with little publicity. In general at that time, such concerns were more inclined to stick to petrol engines even for larger vehicles, but there were exceptions. Other cases may have been demonstrators or experimental, although vehicles run on trade plates would not have figured in the statistics.

**Conversions from petrol to oil**

Fitting oil engines to replace the petrol units in existing vehicles was commonplace among larger buses in the 1930s, at first often on an experimental basis, though later on quite a wide scale in some company fleets. There were also a few instances among smaller

## ANALYSIS OF KNOWN NEW SMALL DIESEL BUS DELIVERIES 1935-38

| Year ended 30 Sept | New 9-20-seat recorded national totals | Make and model | Operator | Quantity | Year ended 30 Sept | 21-26-seat recorded national totals | Make and model | Operator | Quantity |
|---|---|---|---|---|---|---|---|---|---|
| | | | | | 1935 | 20 | Leyland Cub KPZO3 | Southampton | 9 |
| 1935 | 83 | Leyland Cub KPO3 | LPTB | 74 | | | not accounted for | | 11 |
| | | Leyland Cub KPO3 | Southampton | 2 (airport) | | | | | |
| | | Leyland Cub 1KPO2 | Crosville | 7?(of 12) | 1936 | 7 | (Leyland Tiger TS7 | SMT | 6 coaches) |
| | | | | | | | Leyland Cub KPZO2 | Swindon | 1? (of 4) |
| 1936 | 33 | Leyland Cub 1KPO2 | Crosville | 5? | | | | | |
| | | Leyland Cub KPZO2 | LPTB | 22 | 1937 | 28 | Leyland Cub KPZO2 | Swindon | 3? |
| | | Leyland Cub 1KPO2 | Coventry | 3 | | | Leyland Cub KPZO2 | Crosville | 10 |
| | | not accounted for | | 3 | | | not accounted for | | 15 |
| 1937 | 39 | Leyland Cub KPZO1 | Crosville | 12 | 1938 | 13 | not accounted for | | 13 |
| | | Leyland Cub KPZO1 | Lincs | 30 | | | | | |
| | | (total 'oversubscribed' by | | 3) | | | | | |
| 1938 | 27 | Leyland Cub KPZO1 | Lincs | 20 | | | | | |
| | | Leyland Cub REC | LPTB | 1 | | | | | |
| | | Dennis Ace (4LK) | ECOC | 8 | | | | | |
| | | (total 'oversubscribed' by | | 2) | | | | | |

types, though most operators believed the considerable expense of doing so rarely justifiable when related to the fuel saving obtainable. There were exceptions, such as Reading Corporation's bonneted Guy C-type 25-seat buses of 1928-30, of which it is understood that five received AEC oil engines and radiators in the earlier 1930s.

This practice, plus the possibilities of reconversion of vehicles found unsatisfactory, and withdrawals due to age or accident damage represent some of the traps for the unwary in seeking to analyse statistics of this kind.

An illustration of the need to watch the arithmetic was the way the 16 oil-engined 9-20-seat vehicles in use at 30 September 1934 rose to 117 by the following year, an increase of 101 despite the total of new vehicles during that year amounting to only 83. The 18 extra vehicles appear to imply the creation of more by conversions to diesel during the 1934-5 year.

On the other hand, the total of diesel buses in this class at the end of the next year, on 30 September 1936, was 143, a gain of only 26, whereas there had been 33 new ones in the year, seeming to indicate the scrapping or reconversion to petrol of seven – at that early date, it seems unlikely that any vehicles built new as diesels would have been scrapped, although it is possible that some found unsatisfactory were

converted to petrol. For 1936-37, the increase of 39 exactly matches the new vehicles, and for 1937-38, there was a net gain of 24, three short of the 27 new vehicles.

The figures for 21-26-seat diesel vehicles in use actually dropped over the 1934-36 period before rising again slightly to reach 90 four years later, tending to support the deduction that many of the 70 quoted as in existence at 30 September 1934 were conversions of old vehicles – it is known that there were several instances of such conversions of elderly vehicles made to test or demonstrate proprietary diesel engines.

Perkins was by far the most successful firm among the proprietary engine makers in the conversion of small bus and coach models, a particularly significant early instance being the fitting in June 1935 of one of

its Leopard four-cylinder engines into London Transport's C1, the prototype Leyland Cub of 1934, a KP3 model originally with petrol engine. It ran in this form until the Perkins engine was transferred to an even earlier Cub, C76 (which had been acquired from an independent operator) just before the sale of the latter vehicle in January 1939 – C1 then reverted to petrol until its sale in 1946, illustrating how complex a story could lie behind the figures.

However, it was not until after the introduction of the Perkins P6 six-cylinder 4.7-litre engine in the latter

*London Transport took small bus design to new levels with the rear-engined version of the Leyland Cub, built to its specification. A prototype was built in late 1937, followed by 48 more, completed just after war broke out in 1939. Most were intended for central area duties and after being stored for a time they were used with conductors to augment overstretched rush-hour services soon after peace returned before being moved to the Country Area. Seen here in Epsom is CR43 in company with one of the Cubs of 1936 also originally built for the Central Area. It appears that a changeover of a defective bus is occurring – note the mechanic on the bonnet of the Cub, possibly about to fit a destination blind. Both the C and CR classes were replaced by 84 special Guy GS-class 26-seat buses in 1953.*

part of 1937 that Perkins conversions began to become quite numerous, more especially after the war years. Similarly in this size range, the Gardner 4LK had barely made any significant impact in the small passenger vehicle class until after 1938. Earlier, Dorman had been quite a large maker of proprietary engines. The Alexander conversions of many of its large fleet of Albion 30/60hp buses with Dorman oil engines have been mentioned, though this seems to have been concentrated on forward-control examples, including some rebuilt from normal-control buses which had been in the 26-seat class.

Meadows was another engine maker, better known up to the 1930s for its petrol engines used in several well-known makes of car as well as goods and passenger commercial vehicles such as the smaller Guy models but also offering a 5-litre four-cylinder diesel from the 1935 Show. However, this was of the Lanova-head type, a design which had not proved very satisfactory when used briefly around that time by Dennis for a rather larger engine, and it seems unlikely that any of the Meadows version found passenger applications.

So it is clear that Leyland did far better than any other maker in selling small diesel buses in the first few years of production of such vehicles. Yet the volumes involved were very small, with only 250 new vehicles of all makes in the 9-26-seat range entering British fleets over the five-year 1934-8 period compared to 4,346 petrol vehicles of this size, according to the official figures. So it was a very

*The opposition. The Bedford WTB represented such good value as to make it difficult to justify buying a more expensive equivalent diesel model unless high mileage use was planned. The typical independent operator was also often unfamiliar with diesel engines at that period, but may in any case have made the wiser choice to steer clear and put some of the saving into a comfortable coach body such as this Willowbrook 25-seat example of circa 1937, probably a dealer's stock coach.*

modest success – the yearly totals were actually tending to fall again after the peak year of 1935 – and half a century was to pass before the first flush of deregulation gave the small diesel bus a major boost, itself soon to fade considerably. **CB**

*Alan Townsin, best remembered by many as onetime editor of* Buses Illustrated, *has worked on a number of transport journals, and is currently involved in freelance writing.*

A TYPICAL example of a routine function to which transport journalists are – or were – invited was the opening of a new bus garage at Biddulph. Events like this never made headline news, but they were a truer representation of what was going on in the bus industry.

The late 1950s and early 1960s saw Corporations, the BET group and the Tilling and Scottish groups all opening bus garages and bus stations (sometimes both were combined) in some numbers. Open-air parking was not then widely practised and one could find new garages being built in quite small towns. An example of this was at Biddulph, where Potteries opened a new garage with some ceremony in August 1960. The town had a population of about 11,000 and is some miles north of Stoke-on-Trent and a little south of Congleton.

It was a bit of a border town, which is why the garage and enquiry office was shared by Potteries and the North Western Road Car; the original North Western, that is. It opened with an allocation of 40 vehicles, of which 24 were Potteries and 16 North Western. All the maintenance staff were employed by Potteries but platform staff remained under the management of their respective companies.

What probably made more sense of the garage was that it enabled three existing depots to be closed. The previous Biddulph premises of Potteries had been acquired with the Wells business and were a motley collection of timber and asbestos sheds scattered around a yard, and Potteries also closed the Harriseahead premises acquired with the W. S. Robotham business. Finally, North Western closed its Biddulph garage and moved into this one.

The garage itself was the usual brick-clad, steel-framed structure, with an attractive frontage and a separate fuelling and washing area set back on one side. On the other side was the administrative block with a booking and inquiry office at the front for both companies.

Often what is lying around or parked at the back of a garage can be as interesting as what is on official view at the front. Potteries was one of the first operators to buy the rear-engined Leyland Atlantean in quantity: 35 in 1959, 40 more in 1960 and yet more the following year. But it was the reminders to drivers displayed in the cab of one that caught my eye.

*The exterior of the new Biddulph garage of Potteries Motor Traction. The bus is a 1957 AEC Reliance/Weymann.*
Photos by John Aldridge

'Remember overhang' was one notice, while round the Leyland name in the centre of the steering wheel had been added 'when changing gear pause in neutral to disengage clutch'.

At this time Potteries had its own in-house architect who had considerable standing within the whole BET group after building a new garage (not this one) at a cost of just £500 per bus. The group was an interesting mixture of hard-headedness where money and business was concerned and relative freedom for subsidiaries to do as they wished. Its attitude to down-to-earth building costs was emphasised when one of the directors at the opening ceremony started chatting to me about garage design and specification. He had recently been to see London Transport's latest depot. 'Impressive,' he said, adding that he reckoned it had cost about three times as much per bus as Biddulph. 'Didn't know quite how they justified such costs at LT,' he added.

Another pleasant, chatty man enjoying himself at the opening was the Potteries general manager, one Jim Skyrme, who later became chief executive of the National Bus Company. **CB**

*An appreciative crowd watches as a North Western dual-purpose Leyland Tiger Cub/Willowbrook is driven on to one of the two inspection pits after having been through the bus washer.*

*Potteries Leyland Atlantean cab complete with warning notices.*

# FOTOBUS CLASSICS

NOT TO BE confused with its near namesake Photobus, the Cumbria-based bus photo agency, Fotobus is a group of photographers who look to push back the barriers and explore the possibilities of bus photography.

Membership is by invitation, and the men of Fotobus circulate examples of their work for the others to see and criticise – and the reviews are often painfully honest, something that Fotobus members feel helps them to develop their craft.

The names will be familiar to regular readers of bus magazines, often for straightforward record shots, but experimental work is an important Fotobus feature, and the results are guaranteed to delight and infuriate in almost equal measure.

We asked some Fotobus members to dust off some of their older black-and-white negatives to produce some examples for this book. These are the results.

*Michael Fowler's name has graced the pages of Buses and Classic Bus magazines for more years than he might care to remember. Doncaster-based, he travels extensively throughout the UK and overseas, and this April 1963 offering shows the cream of that year's new coaches on Blackpool seafront for the coach rally there. Pride of place goes to the Sheffield United Tours AEC Reliance which carries the mould-breaking Plaxton Panorama body, complete with low seatbacks – a short-lived fashion. The wood-effect side trim was also, thankfully, short-lived. The other coaches featured carry Duple, Harrington or Plaxton coachwork; not a foreign coach in sight!*

*Robert E. Jowitt's amazing photographs of buses, trolleybuses and trams have appeared in many magazines, and there are several books dedicated to Robert's unique style. Those who know his work well will note that there are no scantily-clad young ladies in view, a disappointment to your editor, but perhaps inevitable given the rain in Spain which seems to be falling mainly on an ex-London Transport 'Q1' type BUT/Metro-Cammell trolleybus, seen in San Sebastian in April 1969 after the batch was sold for further service in Spain and converted for the right-hand rule of the road.*

Above: **Tony Moyes, based near Aberystwyth, is widely admired for his rural views, often Crosville buses in North Wales. These carefully-planned studies often capture the remoteness of many rural bus services and the beauty of the landscape. An ex-Ribble Bristol VRT, now Crosville No DVG573, pulls up Primrose Hill on an Aberystwyth local service in April 1986.**

Below: **A less typical Tony Moyes photo, a kaleidoscope of Crosville Bristol REs reflected in a windscreen at the company's central works at Sealand Road, Chester, in November 1986.**

*An unidentified South Wales Transport AEC Regent V with Willowbrook body photographed by Tony Moyes at Llanelli depot in January 1981.*

Above: *Graham Wise photographed this 1958 Lincoln Corporation Leyland Tiger Cub with 41-seat Roe bodywork featuring high floors and narrow doorways; they were, Graham observes, 'not the most popular buses in the fleet'. In spite of this they lasted with Lincoln for up to 18 years. No 86 is seen in 1975, a year away from withdrawal, at the level crossing in Lincoln High Street, beginning its journey to the southern suburbs on route 14.*

Below: *John Robinson is particularly known for his masterful night photography, but in one of his earliest shots he caught Derby Corporation Daimler CVG6/Roe No 137 in the old dark green/ cream livery at Derby Midland station in the summer of 1972.*

While many bus photographers prefer to stick to summer sunshine, Fotobus members often revel in adverse weather conditions where the poor light provides a challenge. Mike Greenwood catches a Midland Red D9 in October fog taking aim for a Leicester side road in 1978.

Wrexham bus station in June 1981 and Mike Greenwood frames a Crosville Bristol Lodekka among shelters which, says Mike, 'would not win any Design Centre awards'.

Above: **Mike Greenwood caught this ex-Western National Bristol LS5G with ECW bus body working on Inter-Terminal duties at Heathrow in February 1972.**

Below: **Corporation Daimler Fleetlines glimpsed through the abandoned departure bays of Chesterfield bus station, photographed by Mike Greenwood in August 1988.**

**Chassis Code Cracking is a popular feature of *Classic Bus* magazine, as GEOFF BURROWS guides us through the complexities of bus and coach chassis type designations. For the Yearbook he has chosen a manufacturer whose codes were as complex as any**

## ALBION

LIKE MOST commercial vehicle manufacturers, lorry chassis were used to carry bus bodies at first, the earliest recorded being the A10 3-4 ton 32hp chassis of 1910. Purpose-built low frame bus chassis were introduced in 1923, the range eventually included PB24 (14 seats), PH24 (20 seats), PJ24 (24 seats), PJ26 (26 seats), PK26 (29 seats), PM28 (32 seats), PFB26 (20 seats) and PNA26 (26 seats). P indicated passenger, 24 was the four-cylinder 24hp engine, 26 was the 30/60hp four-cylinder engine. All were normal control except the forward control PM28. PFB26 was Albion's first bus with four-wheel brakes. About 1927 the Viking range largely succeeded the original range. The PKA26 (29 seats), and the PMA28 (32 seats) had four-cylinder engines, the PMC26 (26 seats), PR28 (32 seats), PKB26 (26 seats) and the PMB28 (32 seats) had six-cylinder engines and were known as Viking 6. The suffix 26 now indicated normal control, and forward control was shown by 28.

The Viking name went out of use in 1932, but reappeared in 1948 as a rugged straight-framed model, the CX41 with 18ft 3in or 20ft 6in w/b intended mainly for export. This was replaced in 1950 by the 19ft 0in and 21ft 0in w/b HD61 which was only built for two years. In the 1960s under Leyland ownership the model achieved a metamorphosis as a vertical front engined front entrance model – the Leyland 0.370-engined 16ft 1in w/b VK41; the 401-engined 12ft 5in w/b VK55CY and the similar VK55CUL with 20ft 0in w/b. The VK41 had air hydraulic brakes, the VK55 had air brakes. In 1965 the engine, still the vertical Leyland but this time the 400, was moved to the rear with the 16ft 2in w/b VK43. This became the VK45 when given tropical cooling, VK49 with pneumocyclic gearbox, VK57 with Turner gearbox and VK67 with full air brakes. These could all carry suffixes to their codes;

N = Normal w/b, S = Short w/b, L = Long w/b, and W = 8ft 0in Wide.

1931 saw the introduction of the famous Valkyrie name with the PX65 (32 seats) and PW65 (36 seats), reflecting the different lengths of wheelbase. Both had the four-cylinder 60hp 5-litre engine as used in the Viking. However in 1934 a new 80hp 6.1-litre engine was fitted, the chassis were now the PW67 (36 seats), and PW69 (39 seats), the latter by producing a very compact front end. They could also be supplied with Gardner 4LW or 5LW engines. A new Albion diesel engine was a further alternative, though not widely used initially. 1937 saw the PW69 replaced by the equally compact PW141 with the same engine range, and the PV141 with 110bhp six-cylinder engine, still petrol as standard. However, many operators specified the Gardner 5LW for the PV141. A three-axle version had appeared in 1936, the PR145 (six-cylinder) and PW145 (four-cylinder). In most cases, when diesel engines (or indeed other customers' options) were fitted, then the prefix S was used, eg SPW141. The final versions of the Valkyrie appeared in 1938, CX39 (39 seats) with 6.1-litre four-cylinder petrol engine, or Albion four-cylinder diesel, or Gardner 4LW; CX11 with Gardner 5LW; and CX13 with 9.1 litre six-cylinder petrol engine or Gardner 6LW. Apart from the Victor, all previous Albion chassis were built with separate amidships gearbox. The CX range had the engine, clutch and gearbox built as a combined unit, hence 'C'. After the war it was reintroduced as the CX9 with 6.6 litre Albion diesel, or petrol engine as an option; and the CX13 with 9.1 litre six-cylinder Albion diesel as standard. All Valkyries had forward control.

*This South Yorkshire Albion Venturer CX37, with Albion's own 9.9-litre engine and Strachan's 55-seat lowbridge body, was photographed at Leeds in September 1950.*
Alan Townsin

We must now revert to 1931 to look at the lighter Victor range. The first was the normal control PH49 (20 seats), followed in 1933 by the PHA49 (24 seats), and the PHC49. 1934 saw these replaced by the PHB49, there was also a PH111 (26 seats). These were all normal control with a 3.15-litre (later a 3.62) four-cylinder engine. Later in the same year a new 3.89-litre engine was used for the PH114 (14ft 6in w/b) and PK114 (17ft 2in w/b) normal control chassis, and the PH115 (14ft 6in w/b) and PK115 (16ft 4in w/b) forward control versions. The Victor will be seen to overlap the Valkyrie range, so after the war a new range was introduced in 1948. The Victor FT39 (four-cylinder petrol engine), FT3AB (six-cylinder petrol) had normal control and were fitted with the dash at the front so that full-fronted bodywork could be fitted. In 1952 the FT39AN (16ft 0in w/b) and FT39AL (16ft 11in w/b) replaced them; these were replaced in turn with the four-cylinder EN287 diesel-engined models FT39KAN and FT39KAL in 1956.

Under Leyland ownership the VT range came out in 1959. The VT15N (15ft 6in w/b) and VT5L (17ft 3in w/b), had the four-cylinder Albion EN289 diesel; VT17N (15ft 6in w/b) and VT17L (17ft 3in w/b) had Leyland O.350 vertical four-cylinder diesels. In 1960 the Albion engines became the EN355, resulting in the VT15A and VT17A. Similarly in 1962 the Leyland O.370 engine replaced the O.350 in the VT17N resulting in the VT17B . The final Victor model was the 1962 VT21L (17ft 8in w/b), again with the O.370 engine.

The Valiant name was also added to the Albion range in 1931, being virtually a six-cylinder petrol-engined version of the Valkyrie. The PV70 had a 6.03-litre engine and could accept 36-seat bodywork. In 1935 the PV71 replaced the PV70; this had the larger 7.8-litre engine, but could have the 5LW fitted. Since it

was now virtually the same as the Valkyrie, the type was dropped, but revived in 1948 with the CX39. This was a heavy-duty forward control machine fitted with the Albion 9.9 litre diesel engine.

It was not until 1932 that the first Albion double-deck chassis was built, the Venturer 80, with six-cylinder petrol engine, or Gardner 5LW. A three-axle version appeared in the following year, this solitary chassis was named the Valorous 85. The Venturer 81 of 1935 had a larger petrol or Gardner 6LW engine. Those built for Glasgow were classified SP81 (SP=Special). The concept of combined engine, clutch and gearbox was adopted in 1937 with the CX19. The standard power unit was the Albion 9.1-litre diesel engine, alternatives were six-cylinder petrol or Gardner 6LW. After the war the model was updated again with a 9.9-litre engine, becoming the CX37, though initially the CX19 was still available. For instance, in 1947 the New South Wales Department of Road Transport bought a large quantity of the SPCX19W, the W meant 8ft 0in wide. Albion entered the underfloor engined bus market in 1955 with the lightweight Nimbus. (Nimbus means rain cloud, how did the Albion slogan 'sure as the sunrise' equate with this?) The MR9 had 11ft 0in w/b and four-cylinder 3.83-litre engine. The NS3N was 23ft 3in long, the NS3L was 24ft 0in long, both had 4.1-litre engines. The NS3AN varied by having a five or six speed gearbox in place of the standard four speed box. All Nimbuses (Nimbi?) had a four-cylinder version of the engine used in Leyland Tiger Cubs. The complete Leyland O.350 engine was used in the MR11L Aberdonian of 1957. This 16ft 4in w/b chassis was another lightweight.

The export market was the target of the Clydesdale which in 1959 took the form of the CD23NW 17ft 6in w/b vertical Leyland O.370 engined model which was based on the popular truck chassis of the same name. The CD23LW was the 19ft 1in w/b version, and the CD23A had the larger O.400 engine. To allow a front entrance beside the driver, the front axle was moved back in 1962 to produce the CD25 , when fitted with the Leyland Pneumocyclic gearbox this became the CD27, and the Leyland O.600 engine made it the CD29. The final version had a synchromesh Albion gearbox, the Leyland 402 engine, this was the ECD23.

One more model remains to be mentioned, built in 1951 they both (yes, two of them!) had eight-cylinder horizontally opposed underfloor engines. These were type KP71NW.

Finally, whilst we have shown dates of model introductions, these must only be taken as a guide, since the documentary evidence is contradictory in many cases.

Oh yes, for those of our readers with a good lexicon, Nimbus also means a bright halo or disk as well as cloud. **CB**

*Albion's Viking VK43 model of the 1960s was a sturdy and simple rear-engined chassis.*

# MEMORIES FROM A
# SOUTHDOWN
# TIMETABLE

## An interesting choice of holiday reading for MICHAEL YELTON as he dips into a book from nearly 50 years ago

*Seen in Horsham Carfax outside the joint Southdown, London Transport and Aldershot & District office, Southdown No 1414 has just arrived from Billingshurst via Coolham on service 75. It was a 1935 Leyland Tiger TS7 with Harrington 32-seat bus body.*
All photos by Alan Lambert

S O FAR as I know, no bus enthusiast has yet sat *In the Psychiatrist's Chair* to have his inner compulsions gently brought out before a radio audience by Dr Anthony Clare; the results might well be not only interesting but also worrying to us all. However, I have no doubt that any psychiatrist would be intrigued by enthusiasts who spend their spare time reading timetables, particularly timetables from 20 or 30 years ago relating to defunct companies and defunct operations.

Nothing daunted however, in my recreational reading for the family holiday in August 1994, in addition to the obligatory Jeffrey Archer and Ruth Rendell, was to be found a Southdown Motor Services Ltd timetable for 30 September 1951 to 24 May 1952. The popularity of Southdown among readers of *Classic Bus* magazine is well established (see the Favourite Top Ten Bus Operators poll in issue number 9) and

even apart from the hardware and its livery much of the nostalgia relating to the company no doubt comes from its actual operations.

The timetable for the winter 1951-2 cost

Delivered in February 1952, this first batch of Leyland Royal Tiger PSU1/13 replaced the 14xx types on services 30, 32 and 36. East Lancs built the 40-seat rear-entrance bodies on these vehicles.

New in April 1952, this all-Leyland Titan PD2/12 arrives at Horsham Carfax on the long route from Petersfield. It had already connected with services 59 and 60 at Midhurst, and also service 22 at Petworth.

9d (almost 4p) and was just over 5in x 3in with a green cover; on the front was a stylised picture of a Leyland Titan on route 12 (Brighton-Eastbourne via the coast) and on the back an advertisement for Southdown coach cruises for your 1952 holiday.

**One timetable**

At that time Southdown published one timetable for all its routes; the Brighton area co-ordination scheme was still in the future, and the book contained details

of all Southdown services into Portsmouth, where the scheme had been in operation since 1946, but not of the Corporation operations. Separate timetables for East and West Sussex were to come later. Express services were in a separate section on green pages at the end. The timetables themselves were clear, well laid-out and cross-referenced; all in fact a timetable buff could ask for save that there were at that stage none of the detailed London Country-style town maps which Southdown provided in later issues. There was,

In spite of delivery of new Leyland PD2s, prewar Leylands such as this East Lancs-bodied example were still frequently found on premier routes such as the 31. A 1939 Titan TD5, No 238 received this East Lancs 54-seat body in 1949.

The original photo that was 'touched in' to provide the cover of the Southdown timetable for many years. The bus is 1946 Park Royal-bodied Leyland Titan PD1 No 280, and is seen as new with its dark green roof.

however, a comprehensive map of the system in the back cover, showing where connections could be made to other operators, with express routes on the reverse.

'System' is perhaps the key word where Southdown was concerned. At that time it had a virtual monopoly of services in the coastal belt from Portsmouth to Eastbourne and for some 20 to 30 miles inland. It was willing to defend that position with great vigour as can be seen from its reaction to Basil Williams and his enterprises (see *Hants & Sussex* by A. M. Lambert, 1983, for the full story). The principal route, holding the system together as it were, was the well-known 31 from Brighton to Portsmouth (Southsea) which then

ran every 15 minutes along the whole of the 3hr 59min journey. In the west, operations generally ended at Fareham as a result of a 1926 agreement with Hants & Dorset, but in fact there was one route beyond, the 45 to Warsash; this was instigated at the request of Hants & Dorset to counter competition from an independent that had extended its Warsash-Fareham route to Portsmouth. In the east, services beyond Eastbourne, Heathfield and Crowborough were enmeshed with adjoining BET company Maidstone & District, and this involved Southdown participation in another well-known and mammoth route, the hourly 122 from Gravesend to Brighton, which had commenced in 1948

No 266, numerically the first postwar double-decker for Southdown, was a 1946 Leyland Titan PD1 with 54-seat Park Royal body. It is seen waiting in Pool Valley, Brighton, to start the long run to Gravesend on service 122.

All-Leyland PD2/1 No 322 of 1948 waits for the service 66 from Littlehampton at Arundel bus station whilst working on service 69 from Bognor Regis to Horsham.

and took 3hr 9min end to end. In the north, there was a remarkably clear boundary along the line Petersfield-Petworth-Horsham-East Grinstead with Aldershot & District, and London Transport green buses as the most prominent neighbours.

This timetable also reflected two recent changes: one was the takeover by Southdown of Beacon Motor Services (Crowborough) Ltd on 16 September 1949, so routes 117 and 118 (Crowborough locals), 120 (Crowborough-Uckfield) and 121 (Crowborough-Tunbridge Wells) were all described as operated by Beacon '. . .controlled by Southdown . . .' pending full integration which took place in 1954, and the other

was the first trolleybus abandonment by Portsmouth Corporation, on the Floating Bridge (now referred to as Old Portsmouth) section on the day before the timetable came into effect, resulting in its initial replacement by Southdown routes 37/37A/39/39A ; later the Corporation introduced its own route 145.

### Lavish

At this time services were by modern-day standards lavish, especially in the evenings and on Sundays. The postwar travel boom was at its height and the private car not yet widespread. However, these are factors common to the whole of the bus industry. What

*Service 59 ran from Petworth to Bognor Regis via Midhurst. Connections were made with service 63 from Horsham at Petworth, and then again at Midhurst with service 61 from Petersfield. No 359, another bus from the batch of 80 all-Leyland PD2/I bought in 1948, is seen at Chichester en route to Bognor Regis.*

*Northern Counties-bodied Guy Arab III No 502 stands in Pool Valley, Brighton, on service 20 for Chailey, where it will connect with service 89 in both directions as the destination screen aptly describes 'for Haywards Heath, Newick & Piltdown'. No 502 had been an exhibit at the first postwar Commercial Motor Show at Earls Court in 1948.*

distinguished Southdown operations was the willingness to co-ordinate services even when that meant extending routes to points that were not in themselves natural traffic objectives, if by doing so good connections could be made with other journeys: thus the 16 from Brighton terminated at Golden Cross Inn, from which connections were made with the 92 to and from Eastbourne, and the 64 from Chichester and its environs via the back roads terminated at Bilsham Corner, a crossroads giving connections in both directions on to the 31. Further, all trunk services were run every hour or in some cases more frequently, and unusually, nearly every less important service worked

on a regular interval even if of three or four hours and even if operated on only two or three days a week: so every departure on the 67 (Havant-Compton) left Havant at 16min past the hour, although there were only four departures on Monday to Friday with an extra late journey on Wednesday, seven on Saturday, and three on Sunday, thus enabling connections for Petersfield to be made at Compton with the two-hourly 54 from Chichester. The 127 (Henfield-Upper Beeding) had its four daily departures at three-hour intervals, making connection at Upper Beeding with the hourly 22 from Brighton to Midhurst, and the 198 (Hailsham-Golden Cross) again had a regular three-

*Left: Many of the first (1951) batch of 24 all-Leyland 8ft wide PD2/12s were allocated to service 31. However, as the route took 33 vehicles, other types continued in use for some years. No 716 is seen in Drayton en route for Brighton.*

Below: *All-Leyland PD2/12 No 737 of 1952 waits at Petworth, having connected with service 22 from Midhurst before proceeding to Billingshurst and Horsham.*

The driver of a new Leyland Royal Tiger sets the destination screens before setting out on service 36 to East Grinstead. It will connect with service 30 from Chelwood Common at Horsted Keynes. The rather traditional-looking coachwork was by East Lancs.

hour interval between its five departures in each direction, which ran on Tuesdays, Saturdays and Sundays only, and connected midway at Coppice Corner with the 98 to and from Seaford and at Golden Cross with both the northbound 92 from Eastbourne to East Grinstead and with the 16 to Brighton.

A further illustration of the clever dovetailing of services which was achieved can be taken by looking at the 30/32/36 as shown on the accompanying sketch map. They ran almost due north from Brighton on a combined frequency of every 30min; the 30 was every hour and the other two services each every two hours. Apart from a variation in the Burgess Hill area, with the 36 following a slightly different route, the three ran together as far as Horsted Keynes, of Bluebell Railway fame. Here the 36 continued north to East Grinstead, and the 32 bent back southeast to Uckfield. However, the 30 terminated at Chelwood Common Pillar Box, where it connected with the 92 (Eastbourne-Golden Cross-Uckfield-Chelwood-East Grinstead). Not only could that connection be made, but a passenger returning from Chelwood on every other 30 could change at Horsted Keynes to a 36 to East Grinstead, and vice versa. The 92 itself connected at Golden Cross with the 16 and 198, as

mentioned above, and at Uckfield with the cross country service 89 to Newick, Chailey, Haywards Heath, and Horsham. At Newick connections could be made off the 89 for Lewes (19), at Chailey for Lewes and Brighton (20), and so on and so on . . .

**Only operator**

It is also interesting to look, as an example, at the service provided to the small Sussex town of Billingshurst, which lies on the mid-Sussex railway line from Horsham to the coast. Southdown was the only operator in the town and gave the prospective traveller the following facilities at the time we are considering: an hourly service to Horsham via Slinfold (61/63/63A, co-ordinated); an hourly service to Horsham via the main road (69); three journeys a day (two on Fridays) to Horsham via Coolham (75); an hourly service to Petworth, then splitting as two-hourly to Midhurst (with connections for Chichester and Bognor via 59/60) and Petersfield (61) and two-hourly to Chichester (63/63A); an hourly service to Pulborough (connections for Worthing via 1), Arundel (connections for Littlehampton via 66), and Bognor (69); three journeys a day on Wednesdays and Saturdays to Steyning (connections for Brighton via 22) with a further two school journeys to Broadford Bridge (79); a two-hourly service on Saturdays only to Haywards Heath via Coolham and Cowfold (81).

The effect of this extensive network on a prospective traveller can be shown on the sketch map, but as for me, I'm back to the beach to work out how at the age of 18 months I could have got from Hawkhurst to Hayling Island . . . **CB**

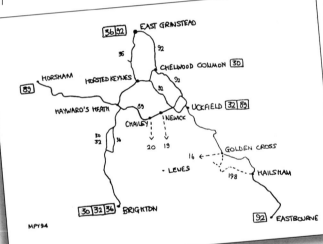

# CHECKPOINT

## No3: Newcastle's trolleybuses

**Born:** 1 October 1935

**Died:** 1 October 1966. History is seldom so symmetrical.

**Initial favourite haunts:** Denton Burn to Wallsend, a 10-mile cross-city route on which 30 double-deckers replaced trams, carrying 16 million passengers in the first year and earning 8d (3p) profit per mile. That was 26% more passengers than the trams which only turned in a profit of 3d (1p) per mile with rapidly wearing out capital equipment. The system was embarrassingly successful, with motorbuses being drafted in as peak hour extras.

**Distinguishing features:** Cadmium yellow, cream and chocolate livery which was brighter than the trams' chocolate and orange and radically different from motorbuses' dark blue. The trolleys' livery changed to yellow, cream and maroon lining in 1946, with motorbuses following suit in 1949. The city's prewar trolleys also were relatively unusual – but hardly unique – in having open rear entrances and front exits with electric doors.

**Nickname:** Bunches of bananas. You know, wait too long and a bunch of yellow trolleys came together.

**What was the appeal of the trolleys?:** The figures speak for themselves. But like many municipalities, Newcastle's worn-out tram tracks were only part of the story. The electrical distribution system had plenty of life left in it, there was growing government pressure to curb oil imports and not switch wholesale to diesel buses, and as a large city in the heart of one of the country's largest coal fields, there was a strong element of self-interest in opting for a modern public transport system that used home-produced fuel.

**Who built the first Newcastle trolleys?:** The 60-seat bodies were by Metro-Cammell, English Electric and Brush, while the six-wheel chassis were from AEC, Guy and Karrier. Operators liked to hedge their bets and shop around for trolleybuses, especially initial batches. Six extra trolleys, three Guys and three Karriers with Met-Cam bodies, were ordered to cope with the extra traffic attracted to the original route.

**And were there more?:** By 1940, the fleet had grown to 113 trolleys on six routes covering 22 miles and the council had decided in 1939 to convert all its tram routes, except the Gosforth Park light railway, to trolleybuses. A Daimler CTM6 demonstrator marked the only prewar break with the triple-sourcing policy on chassis, but bodywork became a little more varied, with Roe and Newcastle-based Northern Coachbuilders taking the place of Brush and English Electric as secondary suppliers from 1937.

**Was the conversion completed?:** Not as planned. Some trams were replaced by motorbuses and plans to convert the Elswick Road route in 1942, with 20 new Karriers, were delayed until June 1944 and were only achieved by modifying the route to save erecting the desired number of overhead support poles and by accepting a motley selection of 13 two-axle, one-door (rear) utility Karriers, 10 of Bradford's cast-off 1929-32 English Electric veterans and some borrowed rolling stock from Bournemouth and Brighton. But the city was still dreaming of miles of double wires as peace returned.

**Such as?:** Parliamentary powers were granted in 1946 for the network to be expanded to 44.5 miles, replacing motorbuses as well as trams and including a never-to-be-seen four or five-road layout at Gosforth Park racecourse. Not only that, but BET's Gateshead & District secured powers to replace its trams

with trolleybuses and went so far as to order 83 four-wheel 56-seaters, contemplate having several low bridges raised and entertain the idea of selling out to Gateshead Corporation which expected, quite rightly, that sooner or later local government reorganisation would unite it to its larger neighbour north of the Tyne. Acute shortages of postwar trolleys put paid to the scheme and Gateshead's trams were replaced by Leyland PD2s in 1951.

**And Newcastle's postwar expansion?:** Most of it was completed by 1950, as the last trams were withdrawn, but some minor extensions followed, the last in 1958 when just over 37 miles had been wired up. These investments and fleet renewal required another 186 trolleys, all with just the open rear platforms accepted during the war. These were a mix of four and six-wheel Sunbeams (Karrier/Guy by their postwar name) and BUTs (AECs built by Leyland) with Metro-Cammell and Northern Coachbuilders bodies. Of the 70 Met-Cam six-wheel BUTs, the first 20 were to London Transport 'Q1' specification, right down to the destination boxes, while the very last – No 628 – was at the 1950 Earls Court commercial vehicle show.

**Where did this put it in the national trolleybus pecking order?:** Well behind London Transport which peaked at 1,764 vehicles, but not far behind Belfast, the UK's second largest system, which peaked at 245 trolleys and 36 route miles in 1953, was cutting back in 1958 and had 215 vehicles in 1959. By then, Glasgow's fleet of 194 was next in the league with 43 route miles (32 of them on the streets), but Newcastle can't have been more than a vehicle or two behind with a system that covered a greater proportion of the city than Glasgow's entirely postwar network ever managed.

**Who killed Newcastle's trolleys?:** If you want a modern day villain, try council leader T. Dan Smith. The subsequently disgraced 'Mr Newcastle' was the driving force behind the city's redevelopment in the 1960s and plans for major road realignments hardly fitted very well with fixed route trolleybuses. The city engineer's office didn't much like them, either. So a decision was taken in January 1963 that they should all go to the great turning loop in the sky within five years. And, as we said at the beginning, that target was beaten by nearly two years, with half the survivors gone by the end of 1964.

**The last routes:** East-west services 35, 35A and 35C. Last trolley of all, on route 35, was 1950 Met-Cam BUT No 599, one of 31 kept to the end. New Atlanteans took their place. **ALM**

*Twilight in Jesmond Dene, with Newcastle no.522, a Sunbeam S7/Northern Coachbuilders, in 1963.*
Michael Dryhurst

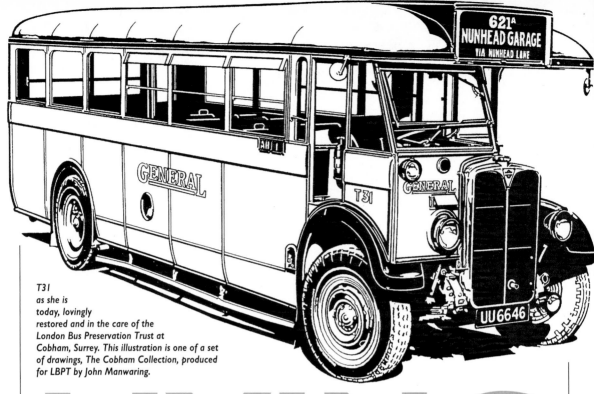

T31
as she is
today, lovingly
restored and in the care of the
London Bus Preservation Trust at
Cobham, Surrey. This illustration is one of a set
of drawings, The Cobham Collection, produced
for LBPT by John Manwaring.

# LIVING WITH T31

## ALAN BOND describes the trials and tribulations when you preserve a 69-year old bus

ONE OF my boyhood ambitions was to drive a London General bus of the late 1920s. Those rugged and racy-looking T, ST and LT- class buses fascinated me but I never thought that more than 40 years on I would be partially responsible for the maintenance and operation of one of those very vehicles.

Most enthusiasts will know Cobham Bus Museum in Surrey and the collection of London buses therein, and that one of the London Bus Preservation Trust's more recent acquisitions has been that of T31 which in 1996 celebrated 40 years in preservation. Believed to be the very first bus to be bought for preservation by a private

individual, it was acquired by the late Prince Marshall direct from London Transport in 1956. My personal recollections in those early preservation years are of it standing in a car park at Swiss Cottage looking somewhat forlorn and neglected but, fortunately, it has survived the vagaries of time and changes of ownership. Reconstruction was, however, somewhat protracted and was not finally completed until 1979 under the ownership of Norman Anscombe, who decided for various reasons that it should be restored to its original rear entrance condition. It was Norman's wish that the LBPT should have first refusal on the vehicle upon his retirement and since Cobham acquired the vehicle in

late 1994 it has become one of the few petrol-engined buses in regular use in preservation or otherwise and much of interest has happened as regards this unique AEC and now thanks to the LBPT. my boyhood ambition has been realised. It is, however, more than just the realisation of an ambition but rather more in the nature of an education as we all get hands on experience denied to recent generations.

*T9 before* (top) *and after her postwar rebuild by Marshall.*
Alan Bond collection

*T44 in her later days of service, around 1949, at Victoria. She carries the body that was originally carried by T31.*
Alan Bond collection

Our first task was to collect our new charge from its home in Sussex and a band of keen men set forth in convoy equipped with tools and cameras, the better to effect and record the recovery. Our Norman was ready for us and after a slight hiccup with batteries the old lady was started. Allowing a short period for warming up was deemed to be prudent and then a start was essayed, only for our progress to be stopped in less than half a mile as the engine died through lack of fuel. The carburettor was quickly dismantled and the offending foreign objects removed from the system but little did we know that this was a portent of things to come.

Cobham stalwart Bill Cottrell was in charge of the driving and his sojourn in the cab was not a happy one as the journey progressed in fits and starts with lengthy periods of inactivity. It was clear that the amount of dirt in the fuel system was more than would normally be the case and this was put down to a long period of idleness. Several years of inactivity with a half-empty fuel tank had allowed rust to form on the interior of the vessel and with the movement of the vehicle the fuel started sloshing about thereby washing a proportion of the corroded surface material away and into the fuel system. A change of needle valve in the carburettor float chamber effected a partial cure, the larger orifice allowing the fuel to flow a little easier but progress along our chosen route of the A25 was painfully slow and it became rather late in the day before we reached Dorking.

### Change of plan

A minor change of plan was tentatively made at this juncture and we decided to head for Dorking town centre, home of a number of preserved vehicles, as this was deemed a safe and secure place to leave our new charge overnight, allowing us to return and solve the problem on the morrow. However, a phone call in advance to Cobham had a small box of carburettor spares racing to the rescue and these were available within a reasonable space of time so it was decided to attempt to get the bus home in the one day after all. Many hands gathered round and, in our determination not to be beaten, a partial purge of the fuel lines was decided upon. The fuel line from the auto-vac to the carburettor was disconnected and, in the absence of a compressed air line, a volunteer who likes the taste of petrol was asked to blow it through. The mixture that resulted looked rather like brown windsor soup with croutons of rusty metal. The pipes were reconnected and, with fingers crossed, another start was tried and straight away we were reassured that we had effected at least a partial cure for the problem. Our confidence was rewarded by the fact that the rest of the journey back to Cobham was made with only one stop and that was right outside the gates.

Having the vehicle on the premises was, however, only half the battle. Clearly it was vital that the fuel system be completely purged if we were to get anywhere at all and over the course of the next few weeks the fuel tank was removed and cleaned and all the pipes blown through to remove all traces of dirt. This done, everything was re-assembled, fuel was added and a start was tried. Everything seemed to be fine, the engine was idling smoothly, as only a petrol engine can, and there was no hesitation when the throttle was depressed.

A test run to put the engine under load was obviously going to provide the proof of the pudding but we were to be mightily disappointed. The performance was flat and accompanied by much popping and banging and the gradients in Redhill Road were taken at a snail's pace on an easy throttle. At the next opportunity a new tack was tried and the spark plugs were cleaned the magneto checked and the carburettor dismantled and cleaned thoroughly. This made things marginally better but no one could say that the performance was anything like satisfactory. It was clear that fuel starvation was the problem so a change of needle valve was made giving an even bigger delivery orifice. The transformation was remarkable; we now had a lively and responsive bus that took the gradients in Redhill Road in its stride. With such a thirsty engine we had been using fuel faster than the gravity feed from the auto-vac could replenish the carburettor float chamber; had the system been pressure-fed by a lift pump I doubt that we would have had a problem at all.

After a few trial runs we found that the carburettor was leaking fuel after the engine was turned off but a little trial and error established that an extra fibre washer under the face of the needle valve would cure this problem by allowing the float to shut off the fuel slightly earlier. We had, at first, thought that the fuel cut-off tap on the auto-vac was responsible for this problem but after fitting a second (ex-Routemaster) valve in the lower part of the fuel line we found that our suspicions were unfounded and the second valve will be removed in due course.

Having got our new charge on top line our next thoughts turned to what we could do with it. Our normal policy is to run vehicles close to home until we are satisfied as to their reliability. We adopted this policy after the engine re-build on TD95 and it has paid dividends in reliability and the lack of frayed nerves. The same course has been adopted with T31 and for some time most of its outings were no further than Weybridge or Cobham Village. In September 1995 we received a request from Mike Kay of London Pride sightseeing for T31 to attend the launch of a new gas bus. The event was to take place at Chelsea barracks and yours truly had the privilege of driving.

The day started dull and gradually deteriorated into steady rain and then I discovered that the open cab doorway was not a problem but the overlapping windscreen glasses most certainly were. At a certain speed the wind pressure forces the water up between the glasses and a constant stream is deposited on the feet of the driver who just cannot get out of the way. This was the day, too, that I found out just why the LGOC and LT were so keen to introduce a better form of transmission for buses in the capital.

## Superb

Make no mistake about it – the petrol AEC is a superb vehicle to drive and even with the crash gearbox, gearchanging is comparatively easy. Currently T31 has the D124 gearbox with constant mesh engagement for third gear and this helps to make life a little easier in traffic. With the original D119 life would have been marginally more difficult. Even so, in central London there is a lot of gear changing to be done and even for the short period I was subject to the usual snarl-ups and hideously selfish driving so typical of London today. I found the task somewhat exacting and a full working day of it would certainly be debilitating in the extreme as well as somewhat punishing on the gearbox. It is a fact that no driver no matter how good he or she is can make clean changes all of the time on a crash or constant mesh gearbox and this tends to shorten the life of the unit considerably. It has been suggested that the change to epicyclic gearboxes in the 1930s resulted in a spectacular improvement in gearbox life by a factor of eight and the financial considerations alone would have made the change well worth while. Fortunately. the clutch stop works well and upward changes can be made without double de-clutching when necessary and I was even able to leave an RM at a set of traffic lights on Kensington Gore, much to the surprise of the West Indian driver.

The D124 gearbox was euphemistically referred to as 'silent third' by AEC's publicity department but to have achieved the objective would have required a helical gear train and that the AEC unit does not have. However, straight cut gears make nice noises and the lovely tones of second and third gears are clearly audible even in the cab and to my ear at least are very pleasant and musical. We are not sure what axle ratio is fitted but it seems most likely to be of the 6.25:1 variety as the performance is lively, whilst use of first gear to start off is not really necessary even though snatch changes into second are so smooth and easy as to be child's play. The main advantage of the design lies in the exceptionally smooth and tractable 6.1-litre petrol engine. It has both low speed torque and top end performance, the latter lacking in automotive oil engines. For the most part only third and top gear are needed and a change down into second is only strictly necessary if you have to come to a stand. Clearly those who drove this type of bus regularly, day in and day out, would have acquired the kind of expertise denied

*T31 as a Chiswick staff bus around 1955.*
Michael Rooum

to those of us who only sample them on an occasional basis; even so, the change to the preselective system must have been greeted with a sigh of relief by London bus drivers in the 1930s.

### All-day running

The next major outing was for the 'pre-hibernation' display day in October of 1995 and gave an opportunity for an all day running trial. This event was organised jointly with the RT-RF Register and took the form of a wake for the old Kingston bus station which was due for demolition. A run out to Kingston was made at the start of the day's events and the old lady was duly parked in the bus station alongside TD95 and Q83 while the photographers had a field day. Several journeys were made to Esher and back with a handful of invited guests aboard and much favourable comment was made by the many visitors. This event was staged late in the year in order to allow running into the twilight hours, something which is not possible at the majority of summer events. When the daylight starts to fade and the lights come on the photographic possibilities are endless and the atmosphere becomes highly nostalgic. The final run back to Cobham was made in darkness and the interior glow from the diffused lighting system seemed to form a time cocoon. This system was very advanced for its day and gives an air of luxury which I don't think has ever been excelled in a service bus. The major drawback with it is that changing bulbs is a nightmare. At Cobham we have another problem – damp – and this phenomenon plays

havoc with electrical contacts and those light bulbs on T31 suffer badly. Consequently it is a major job ensuring that the contacts are regularly cleaned. Small wonder that they were converted to standard lighting at the first opportunity.

Having an active museum even in the winter months means that we get visitors all the year round and it is our policy to give guests a ride on a bus if vehicles and drivers are available. One cold day in December 1995 we were entertaining Brian Dyes from the Ipswich Transport Museum while he was giving us some much needed advice on museum documentation. After lunch I treated him to a run in T31: it was just a short run to Leatherhead and back but by the time I arrived back at Cobham I was frozen. The open cab door seemed to be the least of my problems for most of the draught comes through the gap between the driver's emergency window and the fixed window pane on the nearside. The emergency exit sits about an inch proud of the window pillar and the resultant gap guides the slipstream in and straight into the driver's face so that what starts as a nice cooling breeze in the summer becomes an icy blast in December. This gap should, I believe, have a rubber seal to stop this draught but with the passage of time it has been lost and forgotten. The cab on the 1T is of a style which only appeared on these 50 buses and, I believe, LT1, after which the design was modified to effect a better seal. Certainly the cab window on LT165, the LT Museum's example, is a neater and better design than that on T31. However, the problem remains and will definitely be remedied before the coming winter.

During the winter months of 1995-96 plans were hatched to attend the AEC Society rally in Nottingham at the end of May 1996. Everything was looking rosy until it was discovered with less than two weeks to go that we had a clutch problem and a quick replacement job was on the cards. The gearbox was removed by our expert technician Andy Baxter and fears about the clutch were seen to be fully justified.

## Expensive

That fitted was of the multi-plate type and the woven plates were found to be oval in shape while the clutch release fingers on the pressure plate were very badly worn. Fortunately we have a number of clutch parts and spare gearboxes and a spare clutch plate was swiftly dispatched for a re-line which worked out to be somewhat expensive. Prices like these make us glad we are a group and not individuals, for, without adequate funds, maintenance alone becomes a problem while restoration projects would take many times longer. At this juncture the opportunity was taken to fit a spare gearbox as the reverse gear pinion on the old unit was markedly worn. While it is not a problem that affects the driving of the vehicle it could lead to premature failure and, from experience, we know that this can – and will – take place miles from home and at the dead of night. This phenomenon occurs with such frequency that we really should have the slogan 'Murphy's Law Operated Here' emblazoned over the main entrance to the museum.

Having screwed everything back together a test run was essayed and the transformation was remarkable. For the first time it is possible on the move to make a clean downward change into first gear every time. This is not an essential requirement around Weybridge as we have but a few pimples to surmount and this old lady sneers at these with contempt. It is nice though to put on a bit of a show for the visitors by putting the buses through their paces and a sequence of changes up and down the box is all part of the treatment. With vehicles of this age it becomes obvious that the carburettor is a crude device for metering fuel to an engine, that on T31 being no exception. There is no mixture adjustment system worth mentioning and thus the performance varies with the state of the weather. In cold weather the engine runs weak as it ingests vast volumes of cold air and on hot summer days the mixture gets progressively richer as the air warms up and expands and the oxygen content decreases. The ideal day for this type of carburation is the summer overcast when there is above average humidity, this

moisture allowing the ideal amount of oxygen to be mixed in the fuel jet for maximum performance and in these conditions the performance is pretty spectacular.

Having got our charge on top line we were ready for the off. Our departure for Nottingham was made in the mid-morning of the Saturday and we bowled along in some style at quite a respectable rate of knots. For a 67-year old bus the miles are eaten up at a remarkable rate, perhaps because it is not strictly necessary to change down from top gear very often, a situation that becomes more and more obvious as the terrain becomes more and more rural. Also remarkable is the fuel consumption, but we had taken the precaution of securing adequate beer tokens for our purposes the better to satisfy the thirst of the magnificent beast. For those unfamiliar with this currency, the exchange rate is 1 beer token = 1 pound sterling and the added advantage is that they are available from cashpoint machines nationwide. Our normal fuel consumption on local trips around the museum seems to work out at around 4mpg but on the run to Nottingham we blasted this figure into oblivion with an average of around 6¾mpg. The run out and back was made with absolute reliability: not a spanner was raised in anger and we were made most heartily welcome by the AEC Society. We met up with an old friend in the shape of petrol Regal JF 2378, which used to be a Cobham resident some years ago and many photographs were taken of the two vehicles together, an occurrence which will probably not take place again for many years.

## Stalwart

Since we acquired her, T31 has gone from strength to strength and she is now one of the stalwarts of our active fleet, currently sharing duties with TD95. All the time we are learning all the little idiosyncrasies of the petrol AEC and we can now respond to her every little whim and foible. The new clutch has bedded in nicely and after fine tuning of the clutch stop the driving is a delight and it has to be said that our relationship is now one of mutual affection. Of course as with all proper buses T31 requires a conductor on the back to supervise loading and to give bell signals to the driver. That individual's duties do not end there, however, as due to the lack of direction indicators extra hand signals are required at the rear of the vehicle in order to keep following vehicles up-to-date on the driver's intentions. I can speak from personal experience when I say that right turns are an exhilarating experience as you need to stretch your arm along the rear of the vehicle while being outrigged the maximum distance possible behind the rear axle which, like the front, has no shock absorbers. The ride at the rear end is very lively indeed and passengers seated on the offside rear seats must hang on very tightly in order to avoid being ejected from the vehicle on the faster right hand turns. The problem is accentuated by the thickness of the seats which prevents anyone with normal length legs

*T31, as restored, to original London General rear entrance layout.*
Alan Bond

from resting their feet on the floor while sitting down. While musing over the possibility of a class six MoT for psv use we looked at the rear entrance from the point of view of an MoT inspector and decided that the lack of any kind of safeguards for those seated at the rear would make his hair stand on end unless some kind of safety rail was fitted. This would be an unacceptable alteration to the originality of the vehicle and it is most unlikely that we shall ever see the queen of our fleet earning her keep in full revenue-earning service.

We do keep her fairly active and most recently for the benefit of a couple of Trust members, we have taken her along to add a little variety at two weddings and her presence has been much applauded and appreciated. Her presence has also been requested at further functions and I think that the photographic processing companies must be getting sick of the sight of T31 turning up on film after film, but while she attracts so much attention we shall keep her running as long as there are people interested enough to pander to her needs. To paraphrase a famous Duke Ellington saying: T31, we love you madly. **CB**

# CHECKPOINT

## No4: Decimal fares

**Born:** February 1971.

**Parents:** The Decimal Currency Board and the bus industry who together helped smooth the introduction of new coins on buses when the nation decimalised on Monday, 15 February 1971.

**So that was the day the bus industry stopped accepting £sd 'old money'?:** Not that simple. If you can remember that far back, you may recall that old coins remained in circulation until August 1972 and for weeks after D-day, as this inevitably became known (and, dear readers, please don't get it confused with deregulation D-day, 26 October 1986, when even more fundamental changes hit the bus industry), shops displayed prices in both £sd and new pence. Most of the bus industry waited until Sunday 21 February before going decimal.

**Pourquoi mes amis, as one might say pretentiously in French?:** Because only some of the new coins came into circulation before D-day. As early as 1968, newly-minted shilling and two shilling coins were issued as 5p and 10p pieces and the old versions continued in use. The 50p coin replaced the ten-shilling note in 1969 when, in the style of language only a quango of the status of the Decimal Currency Board could achieve, the old halfpenny (worth about a quarter of a new penny) was 'demonetised'. In other words, it ceased to be legal tender. The new bronze halfpenny, penny and two pence coins (worth 1.2, 2.4 and 4.8 old pennies respectively) didn't hit the nation's purses until the morning of D-day. Imagine the confusion if bus drivers and conductors were going to be confronted with change-less passengers on the first morning.

**But you said most of the industry changed then. Who didn't?:** Kingston upon Hull Corporation Transport, for one. This was the city, don't forget, that ran its own phone system while the rest of the nation used what still was Post Office Telephones.

**You mean Hull stuck to old money or started its own currency?:** We wouldn't put it past those proud East Riding folk, but no, they weren't that radical.

**Go on:** KHCT plunged straight into decimal fares on D-day. As early as July 1969, it had trailblazed for the industry by working with Bell Punch to develop the 'no change' Autofare system, using sealed coin vaults and electric ticket machines. The idea was to speed the introduction and operation of one-person buses by removing drivers' responsibility for handling and issuing change. It already had a system for passengers to claim back overpaid fares – they could get cash three or more days after the event by presenting a special ticket at the corporation offices, or else they could get it back in the mail by postage stamps. With those arrangements in place, KHCT was confident it could cope with people tendering old money.

**And how was old money treated after decimalisation?:** Bus operators (like all other traders) were obliged to accept old coins. If a fistful of them exactly equalled the decimal fare or a higher decimal total, it was all very straightforward, but it could be more difficult if they couldn't tender the exact sum. As was explained at the time, if you tendered seven old pennies for a 3p fare, you would be underpaying, but if you tendered eight old pennies you would be overpaying. In neither case could the driver or conductor give you the right change. The way round it was to insist that old coins could only be tendered in lots of six old pennies (2.5p).

**So what happened to fares outside Hull?:** London Transport, with the biggest task of all, started thinking about it in 1967 and set up a decimal currency committee which then, no doubt, devoted many long hours to deciding a strategy that would be the model for others. Its 15,000 bus staff underwent decimal training and well ahead of D-day it brought in fares on most routes which would translate simply into decimal sums – fares like 6d (2.5p), one shilling (5p) and two shillings (10p) that no doubt seemed outrageously high in 1971, but today sound like bargains.

**Only on most routes?:** By February 1971, the flat fare on Red Arrow and some suburban routes had gone up from an old sixpence to nine old pennies, with passengers expected to pay with sixpences and threepenny bits. There wasn't a direct decimal equivalent, so the new fare was rounded up to 4p (9.6 old pennies), with passengers required to use new penny and two pence coins.

**Sounds like hidden inflation:** It was. Both the Wilson and Heath governments had let it be known that decimalisation wasn't to be an excuse for sneaking in increased charges in any business, but inflation was prompting regular fares increases anyway, so bus operators could argue that its charges would have to rise sooner or later, regardless of whether the pound was divided into 100 new pence or 240 old ones. And the impending withdrawal of the popular old sixpence coin made it less easy to have fares graduated in bands of 2.5p. Today, we hardly blink when some fares scales start with a £1 short hop – but you can't blame all that level of inflation on going decimal. **ALM**

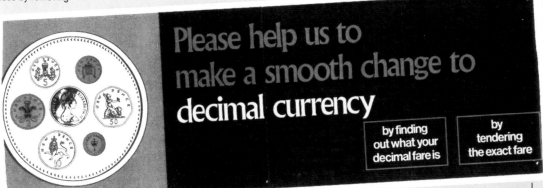

Please help us to make a smooth change to **decimal currency**

| by finding out what your decimal fare is | by tendering the exact fare |

# THIRD TIME LUCKY

**This is the story of a batch of six BUT double-deck trolleybuses that became Britain's only third-hand trolleys. STEVE LOCKWOOD tells a tale of vehicles that were unsuitable and barely wanted by their first owners, non-standard in their second owners fleet, transformed by their third owners into some of the finest vehicles of their time and in service almost to the end of trolleybus operation in Britain.**

*LHN 780, the first of the batch, seen in Prebend Row, Darlington at the Park Lane loading barrier. Although it eventually passed to Bradford it was the only one of the six not to be rebodied and was cut up for spares without being used there. The road the vehicle was standing on was at the time the Great North Road (A1) and the trolleybus is facing London.*
John Fozard

THE STORY begins in 1946 in Darlington, Co Durham, whose municipal transport undertaking operated 67 single-deck trolleybuses on short routes entirely within the Borough. Single-deckers were necessary due to the presence of some low railway bridges over main roads in the town. The operating area was entirely surrounded by that of United Automobile Services – a factor which was to have greater significance 40 years on, but that is another story outside the scope of this article or even *Classic Bus*! Darlington Corporation Transport was unusual in that its services were provided entirely by trolleybuses – a distinction for municipalities that was shared only with Ipswich.

Darlington was an early user of trolleybuses and converted its entire tram system in one fell swoop in April 1926. The system grew in the late 1920s and 1930s but was still confined to the compact Borough boundaries. 24 single-deck Karrier utility vehicles had been delivered during the war mainly to replace the original 1926 fleet. Trolleybuses of 1928 and 1930

vintage were still running even though they were well past their sell-by date.

The stage was now set for Darlington to order its first double-deck trolleys but this was far from being a straightforward event. In June 1946 the Corporation Streets Committee enquired from its transport counterpart whether it intended to use double-deck vehicles in future because it intended to raise the headroom of the low bridges in North Road (part of the Great North Road) and Parkgate (Bank Top station). The transport manager duly reported to his committee after studying double-deck operation in

Newcastle and Sunderland and recommended that such vehicles be used in future. The imminent raising of bridge headroom would allow them to be used on the very busy service 1 between Harrowgate Hill, Market Place and Lingfield Lane which served the LNER locomotive works in North Road.

Thus an order for six British United Traction two-axle trolleybus chassis (type 9611T) with 56-seat East Lancashire all-metal bodies was authorised. The BUT concern was a new partnership of AEC and Leyland trolleybus interests that had only just been set up.

*Left: **Seen in March 1951, LHN 783 is pictured at the Cockerton loading barrier on High Row, Darlington. It too is standing on the A1 road, but facing Edinburgh.***
Alan B. Cross

*Below: **LHN 782 en route to Cockerton in leafy Woodland Road soon after entering service. From Cockerton, the bus would return to the town centre by another route.***
GEC Traction

However, in April 1947, the Corporation, following a review of its transport system, resolved to convert its trolleybus network to motorbuses. This was principally due to the age and unreliability of the electrical feeder network, the increase in road traffic (the Great North Road ran right through Darlington's town centre in those days), and the desire to introduce new bus routes into developing council housing estates. It was consequently resolved to cancel the order for six trolleybuses and to substitute an order for eight motorbuses.

### Intervention

The next development in this saga was the intervention of the Ministry of Transport no less. This body advised the Corporation to shelve its plans to abandon the trolleybus system due to the provisions of the Transport Act 1947 which authorised the setting up of area transport boards. An early experimental scheme was proposed for County Durham and in effect this meant that Darlington's trolleybuses were likely to be nationalised. The order for six trolleys was resurrected (though the eight motorbuses were ordered as well to open new routes into the estates).

Thus it was that Darlington took delivery of its double-deck trolleybuses in April/May 1949. They were numbered 68-73 in the fleet (registered LHN 780-5). The East Lancashire bodies were typical of the period – one interesting feature being the shape of the upper-deck emergency door glazing which followed that on London's trolleybuses. No doubt this was a legacy of the East Lancs trolleybus bodies supplied to London just after the war to rehabilitate bomb-damaged vehicles. Similar bodies supplied a year later to the

Tees-side trolleybus undertaking on Sunbeam chassis did not have this feature.

The Corporation's high hopes for these vehicles were, for the time being, frustrated by inactivity on the bridge front and the new trolleys had to enter service on one of the routes not affected by bridges – service 5 between Park Lane and Cockerton. The route was quite short at the Park Lane end with a reverser across the junction with Parkside, and the Cockerton section was a clockwise circular from the Market Place to Cockerton via the leafy Woodland Road, returning via suburban Willow Road. This service was not the busiest on the system, nor were the English Electric 120hp motors fitted hardly taxed – the only appreciable adverse gradient being the few hundred yards up Victoria Road to the west entrance to Bank Top station.

### First abandonment

As well as no improvements to bridges there was also no sign of an early commencement of the Government's plans and the Ministry of Transport relented to allow Darlington to start replacing its trolleys with motorbuses. The first route abandonment took place in November 1951 (service 2 between Haughton and Harrowgate Hill). The six double-deckers were still plodding away on service 5 (though they did occasionally operate Sunday afternoon trips on the Coniscliffe Road service to increase capacity for trippers to the River Tees). Therefore, the decision was taken to dispose of these three-year old vehicles whilst a good price could be obtained for them and they were advertised for sale in October 1951. At the end of September that year these vehicles had travelled

between 90,000 and 94,000 miles each since new which indicates that, however unsuitable they may have been, they certainly did not languish at the back of the depot!

A buyer did not prove difficult to find and in January 1952 the Corporation authorised the sale of the six double-deckers to Doncaster Corporation Transport at book price as at 31 March 1952. This price was £2,905 each compared with just over £4,000 when new. The heads of agreement between the two Corporations was signed on 16 April 1952 and the buses left Darlington one per day in numerical order commencing with No 68 on 23 April until No 73 departed on 1 May.

**To Doncaster**

We now follow our sextet down the Great North Road for 75 miles to the then West Riding town of Doncaster. Another relatively early convert to trolleybuses, Doncaster commenced such operation in 1928, two years after Darlington, with a fleet of three-axle double-deckers including one of the only two Bristol trolleybuses built. Like Darlington, the remains of the original fleet were replaced by a batch of wartime utility trolleybuses, these being two-axle double-deck Karrier Ws. By 1952 the Corporation operated 46 trolleybuses on six routes (it also had a considerable motorbus fleet) and was looking to replace Karrier trolleybuses of 1933-5 vintage. Darlington's bargains appeared to fit the bill even though, being BUTs, they introduced a new type into the fleet. Doncaster numbered its purchases 378-83 and the first one is reported to have entered service after repaint in dark red/white livery on 7 May. The livery was applied in a non-standard way, the window areas being white rather than the normal arrangement

of white bands below the upper-deck windows and above and below the lower-deck ones.

The buses were used mainly on the service to Bentley which was a village to the north-east of Doncaster. Apart from wiring connecting it with the depot at Greyfriars Road, the route was physically unconnected with the rest of the system. Its town terminus was at a small bus station at North Bridge and, echoing Darlington, the first part of the route followed the Great North Road. It was also service number 1, the service that these buses could not manage to operate on in Darlington. Incidentally, Doncaster had no low bridge problems on its trolleybus routes – the railways there tend to go under the roads rather than over!

From around 1954 Doncaster's fleet policy towards its trolleybuses changed and a programme of rebodying its wartime vehicles was started. More secondhand purchases were also made and all these were Sunbeam Ws (from Southend, Pontypridd and Mexborough & Swinton). These too were rebodied and replaced the last of the prewar six-wheelers. The six BUTs therefore remained non-standard and by the mid-1950s the condition of the bodywork was beginning to cause concern although they were not included in the rebodying programme.

On 12 February 1956 the Bentley route was converted to motorbus operation. This was not the beginning of the abandonment of the system (two short extensions to the system took place in 1957/8, but was because of impending road improvements in the vicinity of North Bridge and the isolated nature of the route. Thereafter the BUTs worked elsewhere on the system. By this time standard livery had been

adopted (with three white bands) and this was later modified for the whole fleet by the deletion of the band under the upper deck windows. These changes meant that the Darlington vehicles would carry three versions of the Doncaster livery.

## To Bradford

However, the writing was on the wall for the six 'Darlingtons'. The completion of the rebodying programme resulted in Doncaster's trolleybus requirements being able to be met by these modernised vehicles – all Karrier/Sunbeams. The BUTs were still odd-men-out and their bodywork condition was relatively poor. In late 1959 they were offered for sale and sold to Bradford City Transport for £500 each. Some had been taken out of service earlier that year and the batch was officially withdrawn in December.

Bradford's role in British trolleybus history is, of course, well known. It was the first and it would be the last. It was one of the largest systems outside London and during the late 1950s it had pursued a policy of expansion and purchasing secondhand vehicles, many of which were rebodied to modern standards. The latest of these had forward entrances and platform doors. Eight of them started life as single-deck wartime utility trolleybuses from, of all places, Darlington and these even had their chassis lengthened to accommodate their new 70-seat bodies. Of 73 secondhand purchases by Bradford already in service at this date (not counting those bought purely for dismantling for spare parts or that did not enter service), 25 had BUT chassis and these joined the 20 BUTs that were Bradford's last new trolleybus purchases. None of these 45 trolleybuses were rebodied.

Our six friends joined a fleet that held the BUT chassis in high regard. The very poor condition of the

bodies precluded their use unless they were completely rebuilt. In the event the first of the batch (LHN 780) was dismantled to provide a spare English Electric 410 traction motor for the fleet. Eventually the chassis of the five others were despatched across the Pennines to Blackburn to be fitted with new East Lancashire bodies.

## Revelation

What returned from Lancashire in mid-1962 was a revelation. The 66-seat bodies had forward entrances with power doors, saloon heaters, fluorescent lighting, bright interior finish and together with the fitment of automatic acceleration there was produced a passenger vehicle that could easily put many brand-new motorbuses of the time in the shade.

Given fleetnumbers 831-5, the trolleybuses entered service from Thornbury depot during July and August 1962. Once again they replaced prewar trolleybuses, in this case 1935 vintage AEC machines that had themselves been rebodied just after the war.

The five settled down to what promised to be a long and useful life on what was now Britain's largest trolleybus system. However, a recent change of manager and the prospect of massive alterations to Bradford's city centre caused a change in direction and it became clear that the trolleybus system would be gradually abandoned. The rebuilding of Forster Square saw the closure of the trunk Bradford Moor-City-Saltaire-Crossflatts service. The Eccleshill service and the pioneer route between Bolton and Bankfoot succumbed due to the recasting of motorbus services in these areas. Again, large-scale roadworks hastened the end of the Wakefield Road trolleybuses to Tong Cemetery and Holme Wood in 1967.

By 1970 our friends were still operating from Thornbury depot over routes to Greengates, Saltaire

*Another summer 1962 shot showing the St Enoch's Road Top terminus of the through service to Eccleshill. This service was withdrawn in November 1962, although No 834 would continue to serve this point when working on the Wisbey/ Buttershaw routes until 1971.*
S. Lockwood collection

via Idle, Wibsey/Buttershaw, and Clayton. They were rarely (if ever) seen on the services operated from the other depot at Duckworth Lane which covered the routes to Allerton, Thornton-Thornbury and Duckworth Lane itself. However, orders for 70 Daimler Fleetline and Leyland Atlantean motorbuses with Alexander bodies were due for delivery and this would spell the final end for the trolleys.

### Reorganisation

At the end of February 1971 the Allerton service fell foul of a motorbus route reorganisation and Thornbury depot lost its responsibility for the Wibsey/Buttershaw routes to Duckworth Lane depot. Then at the end of June the Bolton Road services to Greengates and Saltaire via Idle went over to the diesel. No 831 was the last trolleybus from Greengates and No 834 closed the Saltaire route. For one month Thornbury was left only with the service to Clayton to run with trolleys and this was converted after service on Saturday 31 July 1971.

In the meantime, on 2 May 1971, the first casualty of our five trolleys took place dramatically when No 832 collided with a traction pole at Idle on the Saltaire service. The damage was enough for it to be withdrawn from service permanently. For the others, they would not be required after the Clayton conversion because the remaining operational depot at Duckworth Lane ran only the Karrier/Sunbeam chassis type and it was not worth maintaining a separate stock of spares to allow the BUTs to continue.

Saturday 31 July became the final day for the four remaining subjects of this tale. In the event only Nos 833/4/5 were allocated to service on this day and No 831 last ran on 30 July. It was also, incidentally, the last day of operation for the remaining ex-Darlington

Karrier trolleybuses which were rebuilt from single-deckers. The last journey of all to Clayton was intended to be operated by Bradford's last indigenous BUT trolleybus No 758 but this failed with a lighting problem during the evening and was replaced in service by No 834 which, with No 835 acting as duplicate in front, operated the last Clayton trolleybus journey departing from the city centre terminus shortly before 11pm. So ended BUT trolleybus operation in Britain. The last trolleybus routes of all finished eight months later on 26 March 1972. Interestingly an attempt was made to operate No 835 for the final closure and it did venture out on a test run but this was quickly aborted due to safety defects.

This is not quite the end of the story, for two of our subjects were subsequently purchased for preservation, No 834 by the Bradford Trolleybus Association and No 835 privately. Happily both are in operational condition and do so regularly – 834 at Sandtoft Museum and 835 was latterly at the Transperience attraction near Bradford.

As we have seen, the story of these six trolleybuses has been truly remarkable and it was third time lucky (well – for five of them anyway). If they had been allowed to live out their intended lifespan these Bradford beauties would probably have survived into the late 1970s or early 1980s – not bad for Darlington's cast-offs ! **CB**

*The assistance of the following published sources is acknowledged for the compilation of this article, and readers requiring more information on the trolleybus systems of Darlington, Doncaster or Bradford are recommended to these.* Under Two Liveries *by H. Brierley and D. T. Beach (West Riding Transport Soc,*

The last day the 'Darlingtons' operated was Saturday 31 July 1971, after which the Clayton service was converted to motorbus operation. The last scheduled trolleybus to enter service that day on the Clayton route is seen here turning from Bridge Street into Market Street on its positioning run from Thornbury depot to the city centre terminus of the Clayton route at about 8.15am. Other trolleybuses entered service later in the day due to vehicle changeovers.
S. Lockwood

1971). *Fleet Histories of Darlington, Doncaster and Bradford municipal fleets published by the PSV Circle.* Bradford Corporation Trolleybuses *by J. S. King (Venture Publications, 1994).* British Trolleybus Systems *by J. Joyce, J. S. King and A. Newman (Ian Allan, 1986). Other information has been obtained from Darlington Borough Transport records and my personal recollections.*

*Steve Lockwood has had a long career in the passenger transport industry in the municipal sector and was formerly managing director of the erstwhile Darlington Transport Company. His interest in transport originated from his boyhood in Huddersfield where he became fascinated by the town's trolleybus system. Starting his career at Bradford in 1967, he was part of the schedules team there at the time of the final trolleybus abandonment. After two years' management training he joined the Darlington undertaking in 1976 as traffic officer.*

## THE VEHICLES

**LHN 780 (chassis 021)**
Into service as Darlington No 68, 2/5/49; out of service 23/4/52.
Into service as Doncaster No 378, 5/52; out of service 2/59.
Dismantled by Bradford, did not enter service.

**LHN 781 (chassis 022)**
Into service as Darlington No 69, 2/5/49; out of service 24/4/52.
Into service as Doncaster No 379, 14/5/52; out of service 4/59.
Into service as Bradford No 831, 1/8/62; out of service 30/7/71.
Scrapped.

**LHN 782 (chassis 023)**
Into service as Darlington No 70, 2/5/49; out of service 25/4/52.
Into service as Doncaster No 380, 7/5/52; out of service 9/59.
Into service as Bradford No 832, 1/7/62; out of service 2/5/71.
Scrapped.

**LHN 783 (chassis 024)**
Into service as Darlington No 71, 2/5/49; out of service 29/4/52.
Into service as Doncaster No 381, 21/5/52; out of service 11/59.
Into service as Bradford No 833, 1/8/62; out of service 31/7/71.
Scrapped.

**LHN 784 (chassis 025)**
Into service as Darlington No 72, 2/5/49; out of service 30/4/52.
Into service as Doncaster No 382, 30/5/52; out of service 12/59.
Into service as Bradford No 834, 2/7/62; out of service 31/7/71.
Preserved at Sandtoft.

**LHN 785 (chassis 026)**
Into service as Darlington No 69, 13/4/49; out of service 1/5/52.
Into service as Doncaster No 383, 26/6/52; out of service 12/59.
Into service as Bradford No 835, 1/8/62; out of service 31/7/71.
Preserved.

# OPEN PLATFORM

**Are older buses automatically good and newer buses, by definition, bad? *Buses* magazine editor STEPHEN MORRIS asks the unaskable**

WHAT IS IT about being transport enthusiasts which makes us all hopeless nostalgics? Was it really so much better in the old days?

I spend most of my working life in and around the modern bus industry. I see huge potential in the bus; I firmly believe it can be the transport of the future, given a huge dose of political will and boldness and a change in public attitudes. No longer is it macho or sophisticated to smoke in public places, no longer is it clever to show one's prowess by downing several pints and driving a motorcar; just possibly one day it will be considered smart, cool or whatever awful adjective you might choose, to travel by bus and not by car. It won't happen overnight, but given the right sort of bus priorities and huge investment in some, indeed most, of the technological advances of the last year or two, it could happen. Attitudes can be changed. But there won't, I'm afraid, be a place for old buses, outside the world of preservation.

I'm not suggesting that new buses are good and old buses are bad. Nor am I suggesting that sweeping away every old bus will make everyone suddenly go by bus. My local operator has recently replaced all our 'old' buses with nice new ones. Well some are nice, others less so because they were built when someone high up, in his infinite wisdom, thought brown would be a nice colour for their interior. The sort of brown you find in 1970s Ladas. But to disregard that last point, the new buses haven't made a jot of difference to passenger numbers. By themselves, the new buses have had little effect. They change the habits of existing travellers, it's true, like the young lady who gets on every morning with a pushchair who is now convinced that her bus will be low floor so she no longer folds up the pushchair before the bus arrives. Or the little old ladies going to the local hospital who teeter through the area designed for pushchairs and wheelchairs, with nothing to hold on to. Or the schoolkids who can ring the bell from their seats and can carry on their conversations until the bus has stopped before deigning to get up and amble, in their own time, to the door.

No, new buses by themselves won't solve everything. A whole new package is needed.

Our attitude to old buses and new buses is strange. I may be a heretic, but as a child I had four pet hates. All were run by North Western. Top of the list were the prewar Bristol K5Gs, rebodied by Willowbrook.

They always seemed to run on the 27X to New Mills, and I can think of neither number nor placename without a Gardner 5LW-induced shudder. Close behind were their contemporary single-deck L5Gs. Its lowbridge all-Leyland PD2s came next, though I remember them redeeming themselves by smooth, quiet running and a good turn of speed; I just didn't like them. And finally were North Western's Atkinsons. To me all were old, or old-fashioned, anyway, and in the case of the three types powered by Gardner 5LWs they were rough things on which to travel. As a kid of about eight (and come to think of it neither the Atkinsons nor the PD2s could have been as ancient as they seemed) they certainly didn't give me any sort of warm feeling about the past.

Nowadays three of those four pet hates are represented in the Manchester Museum and I love them all. They're probably better maintained than when North Western had them, and certainly the PD2, restored to original condition, looks much smarter than the heaps I remember.

But to me buses of the next generation were wonderful, and I suppose for many of us it's the buses that were new when we were children that made the impact. There aren't many of them left in service in my case, but I can still remember the feeling of excitement when Manchester borrowed a Routemaster some 35 years ago. I can still remember studying the sinuous curve of the bonnet, drinking in the shade of red which was subtly different from our own, and longing for a ride on it – which I never managed. It's the stuff of dreams. I remember equally well, 30 years later, taking myself out for one of those daft excursions that only bus enthusiasts make, using a Travelcard, and riding out to Stockwell on a Routemaster and coming back on a then-new Northern Counties-bodied Volvo Citybus. Guess which I preferred . . .

No, it wasn't the Routemaster! How dark, dingy and antiquated it seemed compared with the new bus. For the first time I realised why so many passengers condemned to riding on Routemasters every day, 10 years or so after they should really have been pensioned off, actually had justification in grumbling.

That's the practical reality of riding on old buses in

*Bus company managers inspect new all-Leyland Titan PD2s at the Leyland works in 1949. North Western No 242 must have seemed more attractive to them than it did to Stephen Morris some years later. The PD2 on the right is a Sheffield bus.*

service. Yet the soul of the bus enthusiast is rooted in something much less practical, altogether more sentimental, and something to do with the perverseness of human nature. I also remember when I was at college in the Home Counties in the 1970s, and the horror with which I discovered on return at the beginning of one term around 1977 that the green RMLs, and even the odd surviving RT, had been swept away by Leyland Nationals. They were drab, allover green with nasty orangey plastic seats and whined and rattled like only a Leyland National could. Yet only the night before writing this I stood at the bus stop hoping against hope that somehow the inevitable Dennis Dart SLF would, for some reason, have been replaced by a nice Leyland National . . .

It hadn't, of course, and already I could summon up no real enthusiasm for travelling on this three-month old bus; it was swift, smooth, quiet (well apart from an uncharacteristic and ear-piercing howl from the differential from time to time), comfortable, warm, easily accessible – and soulless. Will it develop character, somehow, over the years? In 20 years time will I be all nostalgic about Dennis Darts?

No doubt that character which makes a good bus is different for all of us; maybe it's indefinable, or perhaps we can make a stab at analysing it. For a start a bus has to look right, and while some buses are obviously well-designed, and others obviously not, to some extent beauty is in the eye of the beholder. A well-finished and tidy interior helps, and today's crop of low-floor buses has some way to go before we can consider the interior looks right.

It may be the fact that I have a musical background that dictates to me that buses need to sound right, though I wouldn't claim that that particular predilection was the sole preserve of the musician. In this respect North Western's AEC Renowns have, for me, yet to be beaten, though others come close, not least the Green Line RCL-class 30ft Routemasters when they had AV690 engines; they sounded purposeful when driven hard and sang nicely in second gear. Added to that they had a sophisticated ride quality, seats to mollycoddle the most sensitive backside and nice little fluorescent tubes below the luggage racks to give just the right ambience at night. In smartly-turned out dark green, with their platform doors to shut out the weather, they were all round the ultimate travelling experience.

Still to be beaten for sound effects, in the Morris book, were North Western's AEC/Park Royal Renowns.

I used to wonder, as a child, whether bus manufacturers actually set out to ensure that the bus made a particular sound. Did AEC employ research engineers to make sure that its gearboxes made just the right noises? These would be bright, cheerful people, looking for a bright cheerful sound. Daimler on the other hand would surely use very refined and serious old gentlemen just to get the 'whoop' right. Now, a bus is essentially several proprietary components bolted together, and does the job efficiently enough. The last engine sound which was anything other than functional, to my ear, was the Leyland TL11, though a Greenway we used to have locally could make quite a passable imitation of a Guy Arab and a well-tuned Cummins L10 in a Lynx or an Olympian can sound pleasing, even if it doesn't make the hairs on the back of your neck stand to attention. But by and large that indefinable quality that made AECs AECs or Leylands Leylands seems lacking in a Volvo or even a modern Dennis.

If you're content to be purely nostalgic, think yourself lucky. I suspect – dare I say – that a few of our readers possibly never travel on buses in service these days, and can enjoy the experiences of travel in buses as we like to remember them at rallies and open days. And let's hope for all our sakes that no red tape ever manages to knock that on the head.

If, however, you long for a golden age for the bus that is yet to come yet still have the sort of makeup that yearns for times past, you are faced with a conundrum. Like me, you will have to accept modern buses that are likely to appeal to people who currently drive Nissans and things, that are functional, efficient – and soulless. That's why we always have some preserved buses in *Buses*; it's not for you to enjoy, it's to keep the editor sane!

There's a place for sentiment, there's a place for realism. It's easy to look back through rose-tinted spectacles, and think that every bus was an RT (mind you, if you're a Londoner it probably was!) with careful attention to detail and no expense spared. We forget lowbridge-bodied lightweights of the 1950s, with no heating, no interior lining panels, austere seating, dim lighting from exposed lightbulbs (Ribble I recall used the smallest lightbulbs it could find!), condensation dripping, or even ice on the inside of the windows, the smell of tobacco smoke, diesel fumes and disinfectant all mingled together . . .

The purist preservationist might work hard to recreate that ambience, and full marks to anyone that achieves it. But would such buses be more likely to tempt you out of your car every day than the very best that the bus industry could offer today? It's that sort of contrast we need to consider when we say, 'They don't build buses like they used to'! **CB**

*After a musical education in Manchester and later at Royal Holloway College of London University, Stephen Morris was fortunate enough to be in the right place at the right time, October 1979, to pick up a career editing* Buses*, a magazine he had read since he was nine about a subject which had absorbed him since an even earlier age. He lives in Shepperton with his wife Heather and son David, and still pursues music as a hobby when the world of buses and his involvement at Shepperton Community Church, the Chartered Institute of Transport and the local scout group give him five minutes to spare.*